Reading Acquisition Processes

THE LANGUAGE AND EDUCATION LIBRARY

Series Editor

Professor David Corson, *The Ontario Institute for Studies in Education,*
252 Bloor St. West, Toronto, Ontario, Canada M5S 1V6.

Other Books in the Series

Critical Theory and Classroom Talk
    ROBERT YOUNG
Language Policy Across the Curriculum
    DAVID CORSON
School to Work Transition in Japan
    KAORI OKANO
Worlds of Literacy
    D. BARTON, M. HAMILTON and R. IVANIC (eds)

Other Books of Interest

Attitudes and Language
    COLIN BAKER
Education of Chinese Children in Britain and USA
    LORNITA YUEN-FAN WONG
European Models of Bilingual Education
    HUGO BAETENS BEARDSMORE (ed.)
Language Education for Intercultural Communication
    D. AGER, G. MUSKENS and S. WRIGHT (eds)
Life in Language Immersion Classrooms
    ELIZABETH B. BERNHARDT (ed.)
Psychology, Spelling and Education
    C. STERLING and C. ROBSON (eds)
Teaching Composition Around the Pacific Rim
    M. N. BROCK and L. WALTERS (eds)
World in a Classroom
    V. EDWARDS and A. REDFERN

Please contact us for the latest book information:
Multilingual Matters Ltd,
Frankfurt Lodge, Clevedon Hall, Victoria Road
Clevedon, Avon BS21 7SJ, England

THE LANGUAGE AND EDUCATION LIBRARY 4
Series Editor: Professor David J. Corson
The Ontario Institute for Studies in Education

Reading Acquisition Processes

Edited by

G. Brian Thompson, William E. Tunmer and Tom Nicholson

MULTILINGUAL MATTERS LTD
Clevedon • Philadelphia • Adelaide

Library of Congress Cataloging in Publication Data

Reading Acquisition Processes/Edited by G. Brian Thompson,
William E. Tunmer and Tom Nicholson.
p. cm. (The Language and Education Library: 4)
Includes bibliographical references and index.
1. Reading. 2. Word recognition. 3. Reading comprehension.
I. Thompson, G. Brian (George Brian), 1938-. II. Tunmer, W.E. (William E.), 1947-.
III. Nicholson, Tom. IV. Series.
LB1050.R35256   1993
372.41–dc20

British Library Cataloguing in Publication Data

A CIP catalogue record for this book is available from the British Library.

ISBN 1-85359-194-7 (hbk)
ISBN 1-85359-193-9 (pbk)

Multilingual Matters Ltd

UK: Frankfurt Lodge, Clevedon Hall, Victoria Road, Clevedon, Avon BS21 7SJ.
USA: 1900 Frost Road, Suite 101, Bristol, PA 19007, USA.
Australia: P.O. Box 6025, 83 Gilles Street, Adelaide, SA 5000, Australia.

Typeset by Editorial Enterprises, Torquay.
Printed and bound in Great Britain by WBC Print Ltd.

Contents

Contributors

Claire M. Fletcher-Flinn, Department of Psychology, University of Auckland, Private Bag 92019, Auckland, New Zealand. Claire Fletcher-Flinn received her PhD in psychology from La Trobe University, Melbourne, Australia in 1987. The following year she moved to New Zealand to take up a post-doctoral research fellowship at Victoria University of Wellington. She is currently a lecturer in developmental psychology at the University of Auckland.

Wesley A. Hoover, Southwest Educational Development Laboratory, 211 East Seventh Street, Austin, Texas 78701-3281, USA. Wes Hover is Vice President, Southwest Educational Development Laboratory, Austin, Texas, where he currently directs SEDL's mathematics, science and evaluation projects. He is an educational researcher with experience in design and statistical analysis, as well as research interests in reading.

Rhona S. Johnston, Department of Psychology, University of St Andrews, St Andrews, Fife, Scotland, KY16 9JU. Rhona Johnston received her PhD degree from the University of Hull, England. For two years she worked as a remedial teacher in secondary schools in Fife, Scotland. Since 1979 she has been a lecturer at the School of Psychology, University of St Andrews, Scotland.

Tom Nicholson, Department of Education, University of Auckland, Private Bag, 92019, Auckland, New Zealand. Tom Nicholson started his career as a school teacher in Australia. From there he went to the United States where he completed a PhD in education at the University of Minnesota. Since moving to New Zealand he has lectured at the University of Waikato, and is now an Associate Professor in the Education Department of the University of Auckland.

G. Brian Thompson, Department of Education, Victoria University of Wellington, PO Box 600, Wellington, New Zealand. Brian Thompson worked as a psychologist in the New Zealand school system for seven years before taking up a position as Senior Teaching Fellow in the Faculty of Education at Monash University, Melbourne, Australia. He received his PhD from Monash University, and since 1978 has been a Senior Lecturer in the Department of Education at Victoria University of Wellington, New Zealand.

William E. Tunmer, Department of Education, Massey University, Private Bag, Palmerston North, New Zealand. William Tunmer received his PhD in Experimental Psychology from the University of Texas at Austin in 1979. From 1980 to 1988 he held the posts of Research Fellow, Lecturer and Senior Lecturer in the Faculty of Education of the University of Western Australia. In 1988 he took up the position of Professor of Education at Massey University, New Zealand.

Preface

How do children learn to read? One day, the accumulating knowledge may provide a complete answer to this seemingly uncomplicated but actually immensely difficult question. The contribution of this volume, we hope, will bring us a little closer to that day. It is our intention that the struggles with this central question will be assisted by our attempts at answering several significant subsidiary questions. The first, in Chapter 1, is a logical prerequisite: What is reading? The answer proposed is that comprehension of printed text, which constitutes reading, is the resultant of the skill of print word recognition and of linguistic comprehension, where the latter is in large part common to both the aural and print mediums. The skill of print word recognition is then distinctive to the reading process. It is this skill which is the subject of the remaining chapters.

Chapter 2 asks the question: Are there different kinds of print word recognition during the acquisition of reading? Two principal kinds of word recognition are distinguished and the nature and sources of the information they use are examined in a theoretical framework which yields some tested predictions that contradict several other current theories. Chapter 3 asks: What are the similarities and differences between the way word recognition in reading is taught and the way it is learnt? In Chapter 4 the question is: To what extent does the context, provided by the text, contribute to word recognition processes during the acquisition of reading? What is the function of context in the acquisition process? is a key question raised in Chapter 5. Student differences in learning progress are considered in Chapter 6, the question being: Are there individual differences in aspects of language development which explain differences of progress in acquiring skills of word recognition?

Throughout this volume there is appeal to the authority of empirical evidence, systematically related to theoretical concepts. Neither personal experience nor ideology are admitted as arbitrators or sources of authority. As well as reviews of research evidence on the various questions, new research results are presented.

The seed for the collaboration of the three editors of this volume was planted during their participation in a seminar on reading research initiated by the principal editor. This took place as part of the First Joint Conference of the Australian and New Zealand Associations for Research in Education, held at the University of Canterbury, Christchurch, New Zealand, in December 1987. The editors' research has continued to be very active since that time and this volume reflects their current interests. However, the volume also reflects international collaborations between the New Zealand editors and colleagues in the United States and Britain. While the three editors are based in three New Zealand Universities, they have all received their initial research training in either the United States or Australia. This also means each has conducted research on reading in the context of different traditions of teaching approaches in different countries. The teaching approach used in New Zealand for the past thirty years has been 'book experience' (i.e. 'whole language') which eschews explicit phonics instruction. (See Appendix to this volume.) This is the context of several of the research studies reported in Chapters 2, 3, and 4. The questions asked in these studies, however, are of universal interest for anyone wishing to know how children acquire reading skills in an alphabetic orthography. The book is suitable for the advanced undergraduate and graduate student. It will also be accessible to many others with a professional interest in how children learn to read, whether that interest be as psychologist, linguist, teacher, or teacher educator.

G. B. Thompson
W. E. Tunmer
T. Nicholson
May 1992

1 The Components of Reading

WESLEY A. HOOVER AND WILLIAM E. TUNMER

Introduction

Reading has often been viewed as a *complex* activity. At the turn of the century, Huey (1908/1968) wrote that to analyse reading would be to describe 'very many of the most intricate workings of the human mind' (p. 6). At mid-century, Gates (1949) expressed a similar view, stating that reading is 'a complex organization of patterns of higher mental processes...[that]...can and should embrace all types of thinking, evaluating, judging, imagining, reasoning, and problem-solving' (p. 3). As the end of the century approaches, the complex view of reading continues to be advanced, as evidenced in a landmark report commissioned by the US National Academy of Education (Anderson, Hiebert, Scott & Wilkinson, 1985) that likens reading to 'the performance of a symphony orchestra' (p. 7).

In contrast, while acknowledging the complexity of its components, reading can be viewed as quite simple in its gross anatomy. Fries (1963) has voiced this view, arguing that while reading certainly does involve the host of higher mental processes cited by Gates (1949), 'every one of the abilities listed may be developed and has been achieved *by persons who could not read*...[as] they are all matters of the uses of language and are not limited to the uses of reading' (p. 118). In this *simple* view, what distinguishes reading is that the reader is exercising such abilities in response to graphic rather than acoustic signals. Stated simply, this view holds that reading consists of only two components, one that allows language to be recognised through a graphic representation, and another that allows language to be comprehended.

In addition to Fries (1963), there have been others who have proposed such a simple view of reading. To cite a few, Venezky & Calfee (1970) hold:

Competency in reading is defined by two factors: overall reading ability as measured by a general reading test which, we will assume, taps basic reading skills, and the w-o ratio — the ratio of comprehension of written materials to that of oral materials. (p. 273)

Commenting on the proposed ratio of written to oral comprehension, Carroll (1977) notes:

> ...if the ratio is high, the youngster is able to read up to the level of his language comprehension, but if the ratio is low, one may infer that the youngster is having trouble with decoding or some other aspect of his behavior in the presence of printed language. (p. 5)

While the above passages imply a simple view, Perfetti (1977) has been explicit:

> To understand the development of reading comprehension it is necessary to understand language comprehension and decoding. The thesis of this paper is that the cognitive part of Reading Comprehension = Language Comprehension + Decoding + X, *and*, more importantly, that X is small relative to the other two factors. (p. 20)

More recently, Gough & Tunmer (1986) have argued for an alternative to the additive account proposed by Perfetti (1977):

> Reading equals the *product* of decoding and comprehension, or $R = D \times C$, where each variable ranges from 0 (nullity) to 1 (perfection). We trust that it is clear that by comprehension we mean, not reading comprehension, but rather *linguistic* comprehension, that is, the process by which, given lexical (i.e. word) information, sentences and discourses are interpreted. (p. 7)

This chapter briefly summarises the arguments and evidence that support the simple, two component view of reading. The chapter also focuses on the question of how the components might be combined to explain variation in reading ability. Finally, the chapter closes with a discussion of the implications of the simple view for both teaching reading and defining literacy. Before these issues are addressed, brief overviews of the simple view and the notion of decomposition are given, followed by discussions of the definitions of decoding, linguistic comprehension, and reading comprehension.

Overview of the Simple View

The simple view holds that reading may be decomposed into two components, decoding (or more generally, word recognition) and linguistic comprehension. The simple view does not deny that the details of reading are complex: the comprehension of language, whether accomplished by ear or by eye, is most certainly a complicated process; and word recognition, as evidenced by the extreme difficulty some have in acquiring it, is also no simple matter. The simple view simply holds that these complexities can be divided into two distinct parts.

As important, the simple view holds that both parts are of *equal* importance. This view does not reduce reading to word recognition, but asserts that reading must also involve the full set of linguistic skills needed to comprehend language, skills such as determining the intended meaning of individual words, assigning appropriate syntactic structures to sentences, deriving meaning from individually structured sentences, and building meaningful discourse on the basis of sentential meaning. Word recognition in the absence of such linguistic skills would not be reading: *at best* such 'word calling' could only lead to the proper identification of what would turn out to be meaningless morphemic segments, none of which could be used to derive meaning at any level (word, sentence, or discourse). At the same time, the simple view does not reduce reading to linguistic comprehension, for without word recognition, reading would have no guide for *any* of the actions of linguistic comprehension, and thus, no basis for the appropriate derivation of meaning.

In sum, the simple view makes two claims: first, that reading consists of word recognition and linguistic comprehension; and second, that each of these components is necessary for reading, neither being sufficient in itself. As noted by Gough & Tunmer (1986), if reading (*R*), word recognition or decoding (*D*), and linguistic comprehension (*C*) are each thought of as variables ranging from 0 (nullity) to 1 (perfection), then the two claims of the simple view can be expressed in a simple equation, namely, that $R = D \times C$.

Reading ability and reading performance

Note that the simple view so stated is a description of reading *ability*, which must be distinguished from simple models of reading *performance*. To explain, the so-called 'bottom-up' conception of reading (e.g. the one proposed by Gough, 1972) holds that reading is a serial process where word recognition precedes linguistic comprehension. On this view, word recognition should take place before, and thus, independently of linguistic comprehension, and it should not be influenced by processing taking place at any higher level. Yet there is ample evidence that word recognition *can be* dramatically influenced by linguistic context (e.g. see Stanovich & West, 1983), and this clearly falsifies any strictly bottom-up model of reading performance (for related critiques see Rumelhart, 1977; Stanovich, 1980).

Nonetheless, the apparent failure of the simple bottom-up model of reading performance does not invalidate the simple view of reading ability. First, while the evidence does argue that word recognition can be influenced by linguistic context under certain conditions, an equally strong and empirically supported argument can be made that during normal reading, the more proficient the reader, the less the reliance on context (Gough, 1983, 1984; Stanovich, 1980). In short, while all reading may not be characterised as a data driven, bottom-up process, fluent reading may best be characterised as just such a process.

More important to the argument, the fact that word recognition does not necessarily precede linguistic comprehension in terms of a description of reading process does not dictate that word recognition is not separable from linguistic comprehension in terms of a description of reading ability. Knowing what must be accomplished (the question of reading ability) is different from knowing how the accomplishment is achieved (the question of reading process).

The Identification of Components

Independent process analysis (Calfee & Spector, 1981), decomposition (Gough & Tunmer, 1986), and component skills analysis (Carr, Brown, Vavrus & Evans, 1990) are all descriptions of approaches for isolating cognitive processes. With respect to reading, Carr, Brown, Vavrus & Evans (1990) have provided a description of the goals of such analyses:

> (1) to identify the set of mental operations involved in any given performance; (2) to identify the organization of the operations and the pattern of information flow among them; (3) to identify the means by which the system of operations is controlled and coordinated, including the stimulus conditions, strategies, and capacity demands associated with effective performance; and (4) to identify parameters of the system — of its individual operations, its organization, and its control — whose variation is responsible for individual and developmental differences in the system's overall effectiveness and efficiency. (p. 3)

In short, component skills analysis seeks to understand reading as a set of theoretically distinct and empirically isolable constituents. The decomposition of reading ability proposed by the simple view is focused on the fourth goal of the Carr et al. (1990) schema, holding that individual differences in reading ability will be restricted to variation in two components.

Level of analysis

When considering the components of reading, one must decide on the level of decomposition to be sought. As suggested earlier, the simple view is concerned with the gross anatomy of reading, looking at the coarsest level of constituent components. Such components are those that represent complete, conceptually distinct, systems of ability. While complete systems may themselves have components, the coarsest level of analysis is that which invokes the fewest components representing independent functions, without which, reading would not be possible. Again, the simple view posits two such components, word recognition and linguistic comprehension.

Causal structure

Reading ability can be determined by both proximal and distal causes. Proximal causes are those associated with process components directly linked to reading, where impairment in the component necessitates impairment in reading. Distal causes influence reading ability indirectly, by leading to impairment in a remote component that then leads to impairment in a directly linked component. To take an example, substantial evidence indicates that phonological awareness, the ability to consciously segment the speech stream into phonological units, is critical for the would-be reader who is trying to uncover the letter–sound relationships employed in an alphabetic writing system (for a brief review, see Tunmer, 1991). In some models of reading acquisition, such awareness is not directly linked to reading, but only indirectly linked through its influence on word recognition (e.g. in the model proposed by Tunmer & Hoover, 1992). In such models, phonological awareness would be a distal cause of reading ability because ability in this component partially determines word recognition ability, which, by hypothesis, partially (but directly) determines reading ability.

Note that compensation for encountered difficulties in any component is possible. For instance, the would-be reader who faces difficulties in mastering letter–sound relationships because of a failure to consciously appreciate the phonological segments contained in the speech stream, may still progress in reading by relying on other mechanisms for accessing appropriate entries in the mental lexicon. Two such mechanisms have been postulated. The first would allow word recognition to be achieved through a direct association between visual codes and lexical entries (as opposed to one mediated by phonological coding). The second compensatory mechanism calls for the use of context in reading connected text: guessing unrecognisable words based on the linguistic context provided by those words that have been correctly recognised. Both compensatory processes will allow some progress in reading, but both will finally fail to advance the child from pre-literate to fully literate (Gough, 1983; Gough & Hillinger, 1980; Stanovich, 1980). However, assessments of the components proposed in the simple view must be made carefully in order to discern the impacts of possible compensatory processes.

Definitions: Decoding, Linguistic Comprehension, and Reading Comprehension

The terms decoding, linguistic comprehension, and reading comprehension each have specific definitions when applied to the simple view. These definitions are discussed below.

Decoding

Under the simple view, skilled word recognition is simply the ability to rapidly derive a representation from printed input that allows access to the appropriate entry in the mental lexicon. Such recognition, which accomplishes a connection between a graphically based coding of letters (a graphemic coding) and the mental lexicon, allows retrieval of semantic information at the word level.

Two general types of mechanisms have been proposed as explanations of word recognition. One, *phonological coding*, is based on knowledge of the *cipher* (Gough & Hillinger, 1980), which captures the letter–sound correspondence rules of the language. Phonological coding holds that word recognition is accomplished by converting the graphemic representation of a word (which is a coding of its sequence of letters) into a phonological representation (which is a coding of a corresponding string of phonemes based on the word's sequence of letters) that is then used to gain access to the meaning of the word as represented in the appropriate entry in the mental lexicon (which has already been organised by phonological codes through the process of language acquisition). For English words, the application of cipher knowledge will not guarantee access to the appropriate entry in the mental lexicon. This is evidenced by three classes of problematic words (in English): (a) words with different letter sequences that result in the same phonological representation (as in *night* and *knight*); (b) words with letter sequences that represent exceptions to the normative phonological representations of those letter sequences (as in *pint*); and (c) words with equivocal letter sequences that permit multiple phonological representations (as in *read*). To solve such difficulties, cipher knowledge must be supplemented by specific lexical knowledge, which can only be gained through experience with print (Juel, Griffith & Gough, 1986).

The second hypothesis, *direct access*, proposes that word recognition is accomplished by mapping the graphic representation of the word directly onto its representation in the mental lexicon. Of these two, direct access is the only alternative that will permit reading non-alphabetic orthographies such as Kanji in the logographic system within Japanese. However, in alphabetic systems, either system is at least theoretically possible. Indeed, one must consider whether both systems might be operative at different developmental stages or whether both might be operative at the same developmental stage but employed under different contexts.

Decoding has taken on many meanings in both the word recognition literature and the educational instruction literature. Some researchers use decoding as a synonym for phonics (e.g. Chall, 1967). Other researchers use the term to describe the conversion of letter strings into phonetic codes (e.g. Perfetti, 1985). For still others, decoding specifically denotes word recognition that is accomplished through phonological coding (e.g. Gough & Tunmer, 1986). Under the simple view, word recognition is the general term for accessing the mental lexicon based on graphic information, while decoding refers to word recognition accomplished through phonological coding.

Gough & Hillinger (1980) have argued that for *beginning readers of alphabetic writing systems*, a phonologically based word recognition system must be acquired, for the major task confronting beginning readers is one of accessing the mental lexicon for *known words that have never before been seen* in print. If the novice can derive appropriate phonological representations for such novel printed inputs, then a lexicon already accessible on the basis of phonological codes through the course of language acquisition, can also begin to be accessed on the basis of print.

Lexical access via phonological codes may not predominate skilled reading, such being augmented, as practice accumulates, by a more direct graphemically based system (for a review, see Henderson, 1982). However, such direct access systems cannot benefit the beginning reader, for in order to acquire a direct access system, both the printed word and its pronunciation must be encountered together at least once, and it is precisely because of the rarity of such *provided* pronunciations that acquisition of the phonologically based system is critical if the non-reader is to become a reader.

As mentioned earlier, the component skills proposed in the simple view must be carefully assessed if their contributions to reading comprehension are to be adequately evaluated. Accordingly, to assess decoding as defined above, a pseudoword recognition task (which requires knowledge of the cipher for successful performance) would be preferred to an assessment that was based on a real-word recognition task (which does not necessarily require cipher knowledge for success).

Linguistic comprehension and reading comprehension

Under the simple view, linguistic comprehension is the ability to take lexical information (i.e. semantic information at the word level) and derive sentence and discourse interpretations. Reading comprehension involves the same ability, but one that relies on printed information arriving through the eye.

In both linguistic and reading comprehension, the simple view assumes careful comprehension: comprehension that is intended to extract complete meanings from presented material as opposed to comprehension aimed at only extracting main ideas, skimming, or searching for particular details. In addition, this view of reading is concerned only with comprehension that is based in language. To sharpen the distinction, note the following definition of reading comprehension offered by Calfee (1975):

> I can imagine a situation in which a few words are mixed with pictorial and diagrammatic information, so that a person with a minimal reading vocabulary is able to understand the gist of what is being communicated. If he can show evidence of such understanding, then he can read in the sense of comprehending. (p. 58)

Pictorial and diagrammatic information may indeed support linguistic comprehension, but such information is extra-linguistic in that its understanding does not depend on linguistic knowledge. The simple view does not provide a description of such 'reading' ability.

A measure of linguistic comprehension must assess one's ability to understand language (e.g. by assessing the ability to answer questions about the contents of a narrative passage presented orally). Similarly, a measure of reading comprehension must assess the same ability, but one where the comprehension process begins with print (e.g. by assessing the ability to answer questions about the contents of a read narrative).

Background Knowledge

Assessments of comprehension must also be equated in terms of the level of background knowledge assumed. To take an example, in the general population, if linguistic comprehension is tested by having individuals listen to a passage focused on baseball while reading comprehension is assessed using a passage focused on the technical aspects of computer hardware, one may not be surprised to find that listening comprehension exceeds reading comprehension. However, if conditions are reversed and reading comprehension is found to exceed listening comprehension, the result tells little about individual reading ability, but much about the relative knowledge individuals possessed in these two domains.

Natural and Formal Language

Relevant to the assessment of comprehension is the debated distinction between natural and formal language. Some have argued that this distinction reflects a difference between oral and written language (Olson, 1977). Others, while acknowledging the linguistic differences of text, argue that a natural-formal language distinction is independent of modality (Freedman & Calfee, 1984). The debate will not be taken up here, but it is important to note that proper assessment of the contribution of linguistic comprehension to reading comprehension can only be done when *parallel* materials are employed in the assessments (e.g. if narrative material is used in assessing linguistic comprehension, then narrative, as opposed to expository, material must also be used in assessing reading comprehension).

Oral and Written Language

The simple view does not claim that exactly the same knowledge base used in linguistic comprehension is employed in reading comprehension, for there are clear differences between how language is represented in speech and in print. To take a few examples, the suprasegmentals represented in speech are greatly impoverished in written language; the availability of previous input makes review much easier for written than for spoken language; and the interpretation of deictic terms may be derived differently in written than in spoken language (Danks, 1980; Rubin, 1980). The simple view, however, argues that these differences are relatively minor in comparison to the great similarities between linguistic and reading comprehension (cf. Sticht & James, 1984).

Evidence on the Contributions of Decoding and Linguistic Comprehension to Reading Comprehension

There is much evidence demonstrating that decoding and linguistic comprehension make independent contributions to reading comprehension. Such evidence comes from studies of both disabled readers and normal readers. In the sections below, each of these populations are treated in turn.

Disabled readers

Although decoding and linguistic comprehension are positively correlated in the general population (see below), the simple view predicts that these components will be negatively correlated in the reading disabled population: If one has substantial skill in one of the two components, skill in the other component must be relatively weak, for if not, the result (by hypothesis) is skillful reading and not reading disability. Consider the disabled reader who possesses relatively superior linguistic ability.

There has long been recognition of a specific difficulty restricted to reading that is not accompanied by difficulty in other cognitive functioning. Commonly known as dyslexia, the disability has generally been defined by exclusion, dyslexics being those who have difficulty reading despite normal intelligence and sensory functioning, an adequate opportunity to learn, and an absence of severe neurological or physical disability, emotional or social difficulty, or socioeconomic disadvantage (Vellutino, 1979).

The simple view holds that the reading difficulties encountered by dyslexics, who are by definition linguistically competent, must therefore, stem from a deficiency in decoding skill. In support of the view are a number of investigations showing that individuals selected on the basis of the exclusionary criteria given above are indeed substantially deficient in decoding skill (Conners & Olson, 1990; Doehring, Trites, Patel & Fiedorowicz, 1981; Seymour & Porpodas, 1980; Vellutino, 1979).

Next consider the complementary case to dyslexia: the disabled reader who possesses relatively superior decoding skill, a circumstance known as hyperlexia. A study by Healy (1982) identified a small sample of children who evidenced exceptional skill in decoding but reading age equivalents that were some two years lower than those expected from chronological age. As would be predicted by the simple view, the students in Healy's study evidenced listening age equivalents that were also two years lower than their chronological ages. From the simple view, when decoding skills are highly developed, linguistic and reading comprehension skills will be equivalent, and in the case of hyperlexia, reduced linguistic comprehension will be responsible for reduced reading comprehension.

While not dealing with a reading disabled population *per se*, Hoover & Gough (1990) computed the correlations between decoding and linguistic comprehension in their samples of first-, second-, third- and fourth-grade children. While the correlations were all significantly positive when considering the entire sample at each grade level, the values were greatly reduced in magnitude when the samples at each grade were limited to contain only the poorest readers. Indeed, in three of the four grade levels, the correlation coefficients became negative, and in one, significantly so.

Normal readers

A number of investigations of normal reading and its relationships to decoding and linguistic comprehension have appeared (Curtis, 1980; Hoover & Gough, 1990; Jackson & McClelland, 1979; Juel, Griffith & Gough, 1986; Palmer, MacLeod, Hunt & Davidson, 1985; Singer & Crouse, 1981; Stanovich, Cunningham & Feeman, 1984; Stanovich, Nathan & Vala-Rossi, 1986; Tunmer, 1989). The *general* correlational trends found in these studies can be summarised succinctly: in the early school grades, decoding and linguistic comprehension are largely unrelated; both skills correlate with reading comprehension, but that with decoding is substantially stronger (coefficients of about 0.55 for decoding, about 0.35 for linguistic comprehension). In the later grades, the strength of the relationship between decoding and linguistic comprehension increases (with coefficients ranging from about 0.30 to 0.65); and while both remain related to reading comprehension (coefficients of about 0.45 for decoding and about 0.65 for linguistic comprehension), the relationship with linguistic comprehension becomes the dominant one.

In addition to simple correlations, more sophisticated analysis techniques have been used to assess the contributions of decoding and linguistic comprehension to reading comprehension. Juel, Griffith & Gough (1986) tested 129 first-grade students, acquiring from each indices of intelligence, oral language, phonemic awareness, exposure to print, cipher knowledge, lexical knowledge, decoding, linguistic comprehension, and reading comprehension. Path analyses showed that decoding made a substantial contribution to reading comprehension, but linguistic comprehension did not (with standardised coefficients of 0.71 and 0.06, respectively). Analysis of the test data from the 80 students who remained in the study through the end of second grade, however, showed that both decoding and linguistic comprehension made significant contributions to reading comprehension (with standardised coefficients of 0.67 and 0.20, respectively).

Tunmer (1989) conducted a longitudinal study of 100 children in first and second grade, assessing the children each year on verbal intelligence, decentration ability, metalinguistic ability, decoding, linguistic comprehension and reading comprehension. Using path analysis, Tunmer found that at the end of first grade, only decoding made a significant contribution to reading comprehension (with a standardised coefficient of 0.59); linguistic comprehension was not found to be significantly related to reading comprehension (with a standardised coefficient of 0.10). However, at the end of second grade, path analysis revealed that both decoding and linguistic comprehension made independent contributions to reading comprehension (with standardised coefficients of 0.44 and 0.31, respectively).

In a path model including both nonverbal intelligence and phonological awareness, Stanovich, Cunningham & Feeman (1984) found in their first-grade data that only decoding and linguistic comprehension made significant independent contributions to reading comprehension (with standardised coefficients of 0.39 and 0.26, respectively). In the same study, a series of hierarchical multiple regression analyses on the third- and fifth-grade data sets showed that after the removal of the effects of nonverbal intelligence, decoding accounted for 19% and 38% (Grades 3 and 5, respectively) of the variance in reading comprehension; linguistic comprehension accounting for 14% and 13%, respectively.

Employing multiple regression, Curtis (1980) found that in her samples of second-, third-, and fifth-grade students, only decoding (all grades) and linguistic comprehension (Grades 3 and 5) consistently made significant, independent contributions to reading comprehension. Curtis found that after removal of the effects of nine other variables, decoding uniquely accounted for from 3% to 13% of the variance in reading comprehension across the three grade levels studied, while linguistic comprehension accounted for from 23% to 35%.

Singer & Crouse (1981) tested relationships within a sixth-grade data set via path analysis, finding that decoding and linguistic comprehension (assessed as vocabulary knowledge) were both causally related to reading comprehension after removal of the effects of nonverbal intelligence (with standardised coefficients of 0.29 and 0.71, respectively).

Finally, Conners & Olson (1990) assessed the contributions of decoding and linguistic comprehension to reading comprehension in a sample of 172 normal readers spanning a large age range (approximately 6 to 15 years old). Their path analysis revealed significant contributions of both components (with standardised coefficients of 0.48 and 0.23 for decoding and linguistic comprehension, respectively).

These studies demonstrate that both decoding and linguistic comprehension can be dissociated in both the reading disabled and normal populations and that both components are substantially related to reading comprehension, with the pattern of relationship changing over grade levels. However, the analyses do not specifically address the issue of how these two variables combine in their relationship with reading comprehension, and this is the focus of the next section.

Combining the Components of Reading

In the statements cited at the beginning of this chapter, Perfetti (1977) implies that the decoding and linguistic comprehension components of reading are combined in an additive fashion, while Gough & Tunmer (1986) articulate a multiplicative combination. The two approaches are very similar in that they both posit but two components underlying reading ability. This by itself is a strong claim for it argues (in its strongest form) that there are no other contributors to reading skill. The difference between the two models is relatively subtle. The additive model claims reading comprehension will be improved if either decoding or linguistic comprehension is improved. The multiplicative notion makes the same claim, save an additional restriction: the degree of improvement in reading that is brought about by any improvement in one of the two components is dependent on the level of skill in the other component. To take the extreme example, the multiplicative version holds that no improvement in reading will be realised regardless of the improvement made in one component if skill in the other component is nil.

To appreciate the difficulty of empirically selecting between these two alternatives, one need only note that both hold that reading comprehension is a monotonically increasing function of decoding and linguistic comprehension, save the two exceptions raised in the multiplicative model when skill in either component is nil. Hoover & Gough (1990) were able to assess the two alternative combinations based on a longitudinal data set of bilingual children. The data set contained indices of decoding, linguistic comprehension, and reading comprehension from 210 first graders, 206 of the same children in second grade, 86 in the third grade, and 55 in the fourth grade. The first prediction tested was that the product of decoding and linguistic comprehension would predict reading comprehension better than the sum of the two components. Entering the linear combination of decoding and linguistic comprehension on the first step of a hierarchical multiple regression yielded multiple correlations of 0.85, 0.85, 0.88 and 0.92 at the first through fourth grades, respectively. In themselves, these values indicate that most of the reliable variance in the reading comprehension measure is explained by variation in decoding and linguistic comprehension. However, adding the product of the two variables on the second step of the regression analysis significantly raised the multiple correlations to 0.86, 0.87, 0.92 and 0.95, respectively, for grades one through four.

A strong prediction of the multiplicative notion was briefly discussed in an earlier section, namely, that the relationship between one of the components and reading comprehension will depend on the level of skill represented in the other component. Specifically, the multiplicative notion predicts that the slope of the regression of reading comprehension on linguistic comprehension will increase with increases in decoding, while the intercept will remain at zero. The additive model makes a different prediction, namely, constant slope values coupled with increasing intercepts from a floor value of zero. The results of the regressions computed within each grade level supported the multiplicative prediction: as skill in decoding increased, the slope of the linear relation between linguistic comprehension and reading comprehension significantly increased while the intercepts remained at zero. This provides strong support for the multiplicative combination of decoding and linguistic comprehension.

Implications

The two component view of reading has important implications for the practice of reading instruction and the definition of literacy, both of which are discussed below.

Reading instruction

The simple view suggests that instruction that advances skill in either decoding or linguistic comprehension will promote skill in reading (as long as skill in neither component is nil). The instructional implications for both components are treated below.

Decoding

While language is naturally acquired by the normal child through mere exposure in the context of human interaction, the acquisition of decoding is not, formal instruction generally being required (Adams, 1990; Calfee & Drum, 1986; Gough & Hillinger, 1980; Stanovich, 1986). The difficulty in acquiring decoding skills is that a natural strategy based on selective association (the pairing of a partial stimulus cue to a response), while initially successful in linking the printed and spoken word, has limited utility. Selective association will not permit the recognition of novel printed words, and for the beginning reader, print novelty is ubiquitous (Gough & Hillinger, 1980; Gough & Juel, 1991; Jorm & Share, 1983). As argued earlier, in alphabetic systems, if the child can learn the systematic relationship between the units of the printed and spoken word, then novel printed words can be accessed without the requirement imposed by the associative process that such novel words be accompanied by pronunciations.

Many have argued that phonic approaches to reading instruction represent the most effective schemes known for teaching decoding (Flesch, 1981; Williams, 1985). While there is evidence suggesting that phonic approaches are superior to other methods with which they have been compared (for a review, see Adams, 1990), such evidence does not imply that phonic approaches are the *most* effective and efficient instructional methods for acquiring the cipher.

Further, the effects of phonic approaches on acquiring the cipher may be entirely indirect. For example, phonic methods may simply facilitate phonological awareness or they may provide the child with an overt strategy for generating pronunciations from printed words, this providing the basis for discovering the systematic relationships between print and sound that is embodied in the cipher. In both cases, the effect of phonic approaches would have no direct bearing on the specific character of the cipher acquired.

To summarise, the simple view holds that skill in decoding must be acquired for success in reading alphabetic writing systems. Further, it has been argued that in an alphabetic orthography, decoding (i.e. phonological coding) will allow the recognition of novel printed words, thus freeing instruction from having to provide pronunciations for every novel printed word encountered by the child. While phonics instruction seemingly facilitates acquisition of the cipher (though the mechanism of influence is unknown), the simple view does not hold that phonics instruction is necessary in order to acquire the cipher: What is acquired (the precise content of the cipher) and what constitutes the best method for acquiring it are independent questions.

Linguistic Comprehension

While holding that linguistic comprehension is a necessary component of skilled reading, the simple view does not claim that *exactly* the same procedures used in linguistic comprehension are employed in reading comprehension, for there are clear differences, as noted earlier. The simple view does, however, argue that these differences are relatively minor in comparison to the great similarities between comprehension that is initiated by ear versus that initiated by eye. The commonalities argued for in the simple view suggest that instruction facilitating linguistic comprehension should likewise facilitate reading comprehension (if decoding is not nil), and indeed, a number of studies indicate that improvements in listening comprehension (effected through a variety of training programs) lead to improvements in reading comprehension (for a review, see Sticht & James, 1984).

Literacy

The simple view of reading also provides a way to look at the notion of literacy. In the treatment below, only those aspects of literacy linked to reading will be discussed (for an analysis of writing that parallels the simple view of reading, see Juel *et al.*, 1986).

From the simple view, literacy (limited to reading) can be seen as the contrast between linguistic comprehension and reading comprehension. For example, if one is competent in a language and can decode the printed versions of precisely the same set of words that can be used orally, then linguistic comprehension and reading comprehension will be equivalent. With respect to current linguistic skill, such a person can be said to be fully literate (for reading) since whatever can be comprehended by ear can likewise be comprehended by eye, and vice versa.

Simply increasing the decoding skill of such an individual will not increase reading comprehension as the meaning of any words that can now be decoded given the newly expanded skill will still be absent from the internal lexicon. In like fashion, simply increasing linguistic comprehension by, for example, expanding the domain of known words, will also fail to result in increased reading comprehension unless success in decoding the printed representations of those words in the enlarged domain is also guaranteed.

Treating literacy as reading ability, expanded linguistic comprehension (e.g. through expansion of lexical entries) without expanded decoding skill results, somewhat surprisingly, in reduced literacy as the difference in skill between oral language (linguistic comprehension) and written language (reading comprehension) has been increased. However, this circumstance also results in an increased potential for literacy as linguistic capacity has been expanded thereby allowing expanded *reading potential* (Sticht & James, 1984) should adequate decoding skills be acquired.

Of course, literacy is not static, and the reading skills of literate individuals can be improved. If decoding skills are adequate to efficiently decode any word encountered, then the limit on reading is the limit on linguistic comprehension, and for each increase in linguistic comprehension, there will be an equal increase in reading comprehension. Similarly, for individuals whose decoding skill is not adequate to decode new entries to the internal lexicon, if decoding skill improves to allow recognition of the printed representation of such new entries, then reading comprehension will improve in step with linguistic comprehension.

While the literacy level of an individual can be viewed as the difference between linguistic comprehension and reading comprehension, many argue that the notion of literacy entails a degree of conceptual understanding or cognitive ability that is to be assessed relative to some external standard (Harman, 1987). In this regard, it is important to keep Fries' (1963) point (cited earlier) in mind: the skills of thinking, evaluating, judging, imagining, reasoning, and problem-solving can be found in both readers and non-readers, literates and illiterates. In short, conceptual understanding is (logically) independent of reading ability. That such understanding may develop either through oral or written language has an important application: teaching reading (in the simple sense of achieving equal linguistic comprehension and reading comprehension) will not reduce the problem of illiteracy if that problem is mainly seen as one focused on conceptual understanding. While reading undoubtedly can further conceptual understanding (e.g. learning through reading), to substantially reduce illiteracy defined with respect to conceptual understanding, the overall education of individuals must be considered not just their ability to understand through reading what can be understood through listening

References

Adams, M. J. (1990) *Beginning to Read: Thinking and Learning about Print*. Cambridge, MA: MIT Press.

Anderson, R. C., Hiebert, E. H., Scott, J. A. and Wilkinson, I. A. G. (1985) *Becoming a Nation of Readers: The Report of the Commission on Reading*. Urbana, IL: University of Illinois, Center for the Study of Reading.

Calfee, R. C. (1975) Memory and cognitive skills in reading acquisition. In D. D. Duane and M. B. Rawson (eds) *Reading, Perception and Language* (pp. 55-95). Baltimore, MD: York Press.

Calfee, R. C. and Drum, P. (1986) Research on teaching reading. In M. C. Wittrock (ed.) *Handbook of Research on Teaching* 3rd edn (pp. 804–49). New York: Macmillan.

Calfee, R. C. and Spector, J. E. (1981) Separable processes in reading. In F. J. Pirozzolo and M. C. Wittrock (eds) *Neuropsychological and Cognitive Processes in Reading* (pp. 3–29). New York: Academic Press.

Carr, T. H., Brown, T. L., Vavrus, L. G. and Evans, M. A. (1990) Cognitive skill maps and cognitive skill profiles: Componential analysis of individual differences in children's reading efficiency. In T. H. Carr and B. A. Levy (eds) *Reading and its Development* (pp. 1–55). San Diego: Academic Press.

Carroll, J. B. (1977) Developmental parameters of reading comprehension. In J. T. Guthrie (ed.) *Cognition, Curriculum and Comprehension* (pp. 1–15). Newark, DE: International Reading Association.

Chall, J. S. (1967) *Learning to Read: The Great Debate*. New York: McGraw-Hill.

Conners, F. A. and Olson, R. K. (1990) Reading comprehension in dyslexic and normal readers: A component-skills analysis. In D. A. Balota, G. B. Flores d'Arcais and K. Rayner (eds) *Comprehension Processes in Reading* (pp. 557–79). Hillsdale, NJ: Lawrence Erlbaum Associates.

Curtis, M. E. (1980) Development of components of reading skill. *Journal of Educational Psychology* 72, 656–69.

Danks, J. (1980) Comprehension in listening and reading: Same or different? In F. B. Murray (ed.) *Reading and Understanding* (pp. 1–39). Newark, DE: International Reading Association.

Doehring, D. G., Trites, R. L., Patel, P. G. and Fiedorowicz, C. A. M. (1981) *Reading Disabilities: The Interaction of Reading, Language and Neuropsychological Deficits*. New York: Academic Press.

Flesch, R. (1981) *Why Johnny Still Can't Read*. New York: Harper & Row.

Freedman, S. W. and Calfee, R. C. (1984) Understanding and comprehending. *Written Communication* 1, 459–90.

Fries, C. C. (1963) *Linguistics and Reading*. New York: Holt, Rinehart & Winston.

Gates, A. I. (1949) Character and purposes of the yearbook. In N. Henry (ed.) *The Forty-Eighth Yearbook of the National Society for the Study of Education: Part II. Reading in the Elementary School* (pp. 1–9). Chicago: University of Chicago Press.

Gough, P. B. (1972) One second of reading. In J. F. Kavanagh and I. G. Mattingly (eds) *Language by Ear and by Eye* (pp. 331–58). Cambridge, MA: MIT Press.

— (1983) Context, form, and interaction. In K. Rayner (ed.) *Eye Movements in Reading: Perceptual and Language Processes* (pp. 203–11). New York: Academic Press.

— (1984) Word recognition. In P. D. Pearson (ed.) *Handbook of Reading Research* (pp. 225–53). New York: Longman.

Gough, P. B. and Hillinger, M. L. (1980) Learning to read: An unnatural act. *Bulletin of the Orton Society* 30, 179–96.

Gough, P. B. and Juel, C. (1991) The first stages of word recognition. In L. Rieben and C. A. Perfetti (eds) *Learning to Read: Basic Research and its Implications* (pp. 47–56). Hillsdale, NJ: Lawrence Erlbaum Associates.

Gough, P. B. and Tunmer, W. E. (1986) Decoding, reading and reading disability. *Remedial and Special Education* 7, 6–10.

Harman, D. (1987) *Illiteracy: A National Dilemma*. New York: Cambridge Book Company.

Healy, J. M. (1982) The enigma of hyperlexia. *Reading Research Quarterly* 17, 319–38.

Henderson, L. (1982) *Orthography and Word Recognition in Reading*. London: Academic Press.

Hoover, W. A. and Gough, P. B. (1990) The simple view of reading. *Reading and Writing* 2, 127–60.

Huey, E. B. (1968) *The Psychology and Pedagogy of Reading*. Cambridge, MA: MIT Press. (Original work published 1908)

Jackson, M. D. and McClelland, J. L. (1979) Processing determinants of reading speed. *Journal of Experimental Psychology: General* 108, 151–81.

Jorm, A. F. and Share, D. L. (1983) Phonological recoding and reading acquisition. *Applied Psycholinguistics* 4, 103–47.

Juel, C., Griffith, P. L. and Gough, P. B. (1986) Acquisition of literacy: A longitudinal study of children in first and second grade. *Journal of Educational Psychology* 78, 243–55.

Olson, D. R. (1977) From utterance to text: The bias of language in speech and writing. *Harvard Educational Review* 47, 257–81.

Palmer, J., MacLeod, C. M., Hunt, E. and Davidson, J. E. (1985) Information processing correlates of reading. *Journal of Memory and Language* 24, 59–88.

Perfetti, C. A. (1977) Language comprehension and fast decoding: Some psycholinguistic prerequisites for skilled reading comprehension. In J. T. Guthrie (ed.) *Cognition, Curriculum and Comprehension* (pp. 20–41). Newark, DE: International Reading Association.

— (1985) *Reading Ability*. New York: Oxford University Press.

Rubin, A. (1980) A theoretical taxonomy of the differences between oral and written language. In R. J. Spiro, B. C. Bruce and W. F. Brewer (eds) *Theoretical Issues in Reading Comprehension* (pp. 411–38). Hillsdale, NJ: Lawrence Erlbaum Associates.

Rumelhart, D. E. (1977) Toward an interactive model of reading. In S. Dornic (ed.) *Attention and Performance VI* (pp. 573–603). Hillsdale, NJ: Lawrence Erlbaum Associates.

Seymour, P. H. K. and Porpodas, C. D. (1980) Lexical and non-lexical processing of spelling in dyslexia. In U. Frith (ed) *Cognitive Processes in Spelling* (pp. 443–73). London: Academic Press.

Singer, M. H. and Crouse, J. (1981) The relationship of context-use skills to reading: A case for an alternative experimental logic. *Child Development* 52, 1326–9.

Stanovich, K. E. (1980) Toward an interactive-compensatory model of individual differences in the development of reading fluency. *Reading Research Quarterly* 16, 32–71.

— (1986) Matthew effects in reading: Some consequences of individual differences in the acquisition of literacy. *Reading Research Quarterly* 21, 360–407.

Stanovich, K. E., Cunningham, A. E. and Feeman, D. J. (1984) Intelligence, cognitive skills, and early reading progress. *Reading Research Quarterly* 19, 278–303.

Stanovich, K. E., Nathan, R. G. and Vala-Rossi, M. (1986) Developmental changes in the cognitive correlates of reading ability and the developmental lag hypothesis. *Reading Research Quarterly* 21, 267–83.

Stanovich, K. E. and West, R. F. (1983) On priming by a sentence context. *Journal of Experimental Psychology: General* 112, 1–36.

Sticht, T. G. and James, J. H. (1984) Listening and reading. In P. D. Pearson (ed.) *Handbook of Reading Research* (pp. 293–317). New York: Longman.

Tunmer, W. E. (1989) The role of language-related factors in reading disability. In D. Shankweiler and I. Y. Liberman (eds) *Phonology and Reading Disability* (pp. 91–131). Ann Arbor, MI: The University of Michigan Press.

— (1991) Phonological awareness and literacy acquisition. In L. Rieben and C. A. Perfetti (eds) *Learning to Read: Basic Research and its Implications* (pp. 105–19). Hillsdale, NJ: Lawrence Erlbaum Associates.

Tunmer, W. E. and Hoover, W. A. (1992) Cognitive and linguistic factors in learning to read. In P. B. Gough, L. C. Ehri and R. A. Treiman (eds) *Reading Acquisition* (pp. 175–214). Hillsdale, NJ: Lawrence Erlbaum Associates.

Vellutino, F. R. (1979) *Dyslexia: Theory and Research*. Cambridge, MA: MIT Press.

Venezky, R. L. and Calfee, R. C. (1970) The reading competency model. In H. Singer and R. B. Ruddell (eds) *Theoretical Models and Processes of Reading* (pp. 273–91).Newark, DE: International Reading Association.

Williams, J.P. (1985) The case for explicit decoding instruction. In J. Osborn, P. T.Wilson and R. C. Anderson (eds) *Reading Education: Foundations for a Literate America* (pp. 205–13) Lexington, MA: Lexington Books.

2 A Theory of Knowledge Sources and Procedures for Reading Acquisition

G. BRIAN THOMPSON AND CLAIRE M. FLETCHER-FLINN

Introduction

The skill of reading an alphabetic orthography is a challenge to any attempt at constructing a theory of acquisition. There are several current attempts to meet this challenge. The theory presented here gives different predictions than the others on several aspects, and these predictions are tested in an extensive series of experiments.

In a theoretical account of acquisition of any cognitive skill, consideration of the following is merited:

1. Goals of the learner of the skill.
2. The learner's use of different classes of procedures for responding. The relationships between these classes of procedures and relationships to the goals of the learner.
3. The sources of the learner's knowledge used in the different classes of procedures, including antecedent experiences and any transfer from existing knowledge or skills.
4. In each class of procedures, the relationships between contributions of knowledge from the different sources.
5. Links between the skill acquired and existing knowledge and skills.

The work presented here on the skill of reading is guided by these requirements.

There are two main divisions in the skills which comprise reading: skill of identification of the printed words (word recognition), and skill of comprehension of the text. Comprehension cannot proceed without identification of most of the printed words. It is the skill of identification which is the object of the theory of acquisition presented here. As the goal of reading is the reception of meaning, this theory includes consideration of the identification of meanings as well as the sounds of print words. The concern is to account for learning that is common among normal readers, irrespective of their individual rates of learning. No attempt will be made to account for individual differences in rates of learning. Such matters receive attention in this volume in Chapter 6 by Tunmer and Hoover.

Procedures and Sources of Knowledge

Procedures for Reading. In this theory there are two classes of procedures for making identification responses to a printed word: (a) Recall, (b) Generation. The first is recall from representations which are stored as a consequence of experience with the particular print word. The second class of procedures, generation, does not depend on experience of the stimulus print word. They are procedures which have some generality beyond a specific word and can generate a response to a print word where none is attainable by recall. Procedures based on letter–sound correspondence knowledge have been commonly proposed for generation of reading responses. For example, by using knowledge of the sound which corresponds to each successive letter (or letter group) of the print stimulus these procedures can provide a response when the reader has had no previous experience of the stimulus. However, other knowledge bases for generation are feasible, such as information abstracted from the stored experiences of several print words. These will be considered subsequently under the rubric 'sublexical relations'.

Sources of Knowledge. While knowledge bases are usually specified in current theories of acquisition of reading, little attention is given to the sources of knowledge bases, or the processes by which they came to be stored. The nature of the experiential history that comprises these sources is not usually specified. It is a presupposition of this chapter that theoretical understanding of the acquisition of reading cannot be complete without determining the sources of knowledge which are used in each class of procedures for reading.

The classes of sources of knowledge in the present theory are shown in Figure 1, marked (1) to (5). For all sources except (3) they are classes of antecedent experiences. They are the sources of currently stored knowledge, the various types of which are shown in the second column of Figure 1. This depiction is not the same as information processing descriptions which show the flow of information from stimulus input to response output. The four source classes (1), (2), (4), (5) are categories of past experiences which have provided the various types of currently stored knowledge, some of which will be activated by the stimulus input and contribute to the procedures for responding.

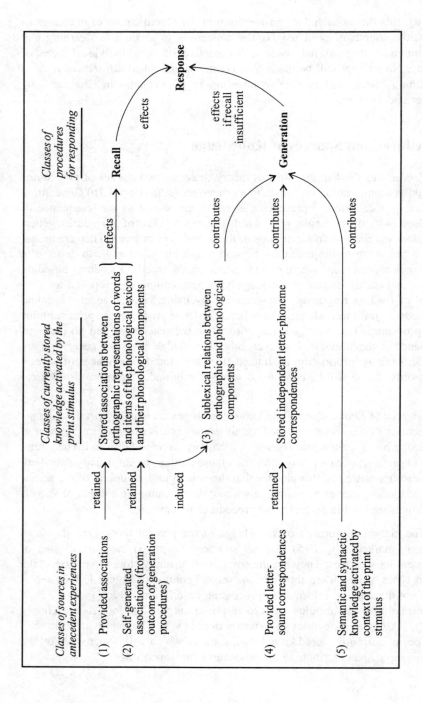

Figure 1 Outline of the theory of reading acquisition: Classes of the learner's sources of stored knowledge, and procedures.

Sources of knowledge for recall

The class of currently stored knowledge which is used for recall is the stored representation of the sequence of letters which comprise the print word and the associations with the (lexical) phonological and semantic representations of the word. The antecedent experiences which were the sources of such associations for recall are of two classes: provided associations and self-generated associations. See Figure 1.

Provided Associations for Recall. In provided associations an external agent such as a teacher or parent provides the child with the appropriate associated experience of sound and meaning of the word when the child encounters the print word. For example, the teacher says *bag* when the child sees the print item 'bag'. Hearing *bag* will also enable the child to access a meaning for the print word. The provided association may also take less direct forms such as the teacher's correction of the child's erroneous reading response. For example, the child reads *dog* for the print item 'bag'. The teacher provides the correction *bag*. It should be noted that these are provided associations, not merely provided responses. The child processes and retains information from the print stimulus and the association between this information and the lexical, phonological and semantic representations.

Self-generated Associations for Recall. Reading responses which are the outcome of generation procedures are the second source of associations for recall. These self-generated associations are a class of past experiences which may be retained as stored knowledge and recalled in procedures the same as those used for provided associations. For example, the child may, through knowledge of letter-phoneme correspondences such as 'b' → /b/, 'a' → /æ/, and 'g'→ /g/, generate the correct response /bæg/ for the print stimulus 'bag'. If this generated association is retained in memory, on a subsequent occasion when the print word 'bag' is again a stimulus, recall procedures will be sufficient to provide the response /bæg/ without again using generation procedures. Retention will depend on some re-occurrence of the stimulus, along with consistency in any generation of the same response on re-appearance of the stimulus. In this example the correct association was generated and stored as an association available for recall. Sometimes erroneous associations may be generated and stored. Some implications of these cases are considered in the next section.

Procedures of recall and generation

Reasons for Two Classes of Procedures. Why does the learner acquire a processing system using both recall and generation? The learner has the goal not only to acquire knowledge but to maximise that which is veridical among knowledge acquired. Recall of associations provided by external agents, such as teacher or parent, should achieve this better than self-generation which would be more prone to errors of veridicality. But the learner's goal of maximising veridical knowledge is constrained by another goal, that of being able to function independently of current assistance from external agents. It is this goal which requires the learner to acquire a procedure for generation of responses.

It may be noted that in the present theory the identity of the source, as a provided or as a generated association, is retained in the stored representations of the associations. (This does not mean, however, that in recall based on these representations the reader has conscious awareness of this identity; only that it is retained implicitly). If the reader is unable to maintain this identity of category of sources the reader will be at a disadvantage in achieving the goals of veridical knowledge. It is an advantage if stored representations of provided associations override stored representations from generated associations where these are different.

The Relationship Between Generation and Recall Procedures. Following the reader's attention to the print word stimulus, both generation and recall procedures will operate, but certain goals and conditions will govern which procedures actually result in activation of the reading response. As one of the reader's goals is maximisation of veridical knowledge, reading responses will be activated by recall procedures whenever these are sufficient. Recall is sufficient if an association can be recalled, and if it is unambiguous in so far as no more than one association is recalled when only one is warranted for the reading response. In the case of insufficient recall, the generation procedures which are also operating will be drawn upon to activate a response. Thus reading responses which are the result of recall procedures will take precedence in time over those which draw on generation procedures. One consequence of this relationship between recall and generation procedures is that the time to execute reading responses made by generation procedures will be greater than for those made by recall.

When attempting to make a reading response by generation procedures, the goal of maximising veridical knowledge will require that the generated (phonological) item be checked against existing knowledge, namely the phonological representations of the learner's speaking–listening vocabulary. This 'lexical check' is a check against the reader's existing phonological lexicon. Generation procedures depend on generalised relationships between orthography and sublexical phonology, not on experience of the particular *print* word. Hence if the print word stimulus has a regular spelling (e.g. 'stop') the item generated in response to this stimulus is likely to be a closer match to an existing item of the reader's phonological lexicon than would be the case with an irregularly spelt item (e.g. 'both'). The closer the match, the more quickly will this 'lexical check' be carried out and the generated item confirmed as a (phonological) word known to the reader. Thus generated responses to regularly spelt words will be faster than to irregularly spelt words. But recalled reading responses to regularly spelt words will be neither faster nor slower than to irregularly spelt words. In recall, a stored association specific to the stimulus print word is accessed. This procedure does not entail differences between words of regular and irregular spellings. However, it does, as noted previously, lead to faster reading responses than the generation procedure.

The present theory thus provides an explanation for the established findings that adult readers' response times for naming regular words are faster than for irregular words when the words are of low frequency, that is, when unfamiliar. No such 'regularity effects' are obtained with more familiar high frequency words, which yield faster reading responses than low frequency words (Seidenberg, 1985; Patterson & Coltheart, 1987). A similar pattern of results has been obtained for accuracy of reading by children (Backman et al., 1984; Waters et al., 1984; Holligan & Johnston, 1988).

Comparison with Other Theories. The present theory contrasts with several developmental theories of reading acquisition (Marsh et al., 1981; Frith, 1985; Seymour & MacGregor, 1984; Seymour, 1990). Included in all these theories is the 'developmental phase' notion that there is a phase in the child's acquisition of reading during which reading responses can be generated (by letter-phoneme correspondences) and that only subsequent to this phase are reading responses made by the recall procedures. The present theory is in sharp contrast, in so far as generation and recall procedures are not considered as belonging to phases or successive periods of development. They are contemporaneous; both can function virtually at any time during acquisition and indeed also for mature readers. However, for all readers, responses to familiar print words will be made as an outcome of recall procedures, not from generation procedures.

It should be noted that the present theory is not a version of 'dual route' theory (Baron, 1977; Coltheart, 1978, 1980; McCusker et al., 1981). Generation and recall procedures described here are not the functionally independent 'phonological mediation' and 'direct lexical access' routes of dual route theory. Generation procedures include sublexical relations which are induced by the learner from stored experience of print words. These relations are a source of knowledge for generation. This link between phonological mediation and infor- mation based on print word experience is not found in dual route theory. There is a reason for this difference. Dual route theory is concerned with the stored representations of information for reading and retrieval of that information. It has no explicit concern with how the representations came to be stored. Such sources of knowledge are a principal concern of the present theory. This is seen in the theoretical specifications on generation which follow. These give rise to some predictions that are different from several current theories which do have a concern with acquisition. Experimental tests of these predictions are reported. In the final main section of this chapter recall procedures are considered. It is shown that these cannot be equated with 'direct lexical access', as access is often via the reader's phonological lexicon, accompanied where necessary by a 'spelling check' procedure.

Generation

Knowledge sources and procedures for generation

The experiential history of the learner may provide three classes of sources of knowledge which contribute to generation procedures for reading responses: (a) Sublexical relations between orthographic and phonological components of words. These relations are formed by induction from stored knowledge of print words and their phonological components; (b) Provided letter-sound correspondences; (c) Semantic and syntactic context of the stimulus word. See (3), (4) and (5) in Figure 1.

Semantic and Syntactic Context. This context of the print stimulus will be a source of knowledge that contributes to generation of reading responses for readers exposed to texts from which they can extract some meaning. The meaning and sentence structure of the text will constrain candidate responses to the stimulus word for which the reader is generating a response, the reader's knowledge having been insufficient for recall procedures to produce a response. For example, the print stimulus word may be 'box' in the following context: 'The boy jumped off the box'. To generate a response to the item 'box' in this context a major constraint is that the response belongs to the set of noun words which plausibly denote an object from which a boy can jump.

Context is a source which during learning will normally be used in conjunction with one or both of the other classes of sources, (a), (b), listed above. It is important to note in the present theory that while context will contribute to generation of a response it has no part in influencing recall of responses. Recall, however, will normally be the procedure for the majority of responses by a reader. Many experimental studies of adult readers have shown that context has an influence on word identification when information from the stimulus is very limited, such as in very brief stimulus exposure. Under normal reading conditions, however, context has little influence on word identification performance (Mitchell, 1982: 108f; Rayner & Pollatsek, 1989: 226f). This is also considered to be the case for children reading familiar words (Perfetti, 1985; Stanovich, 1986). Where the stimulus information is very limited, recall is likely to be insufficient in so far as several different recall responses may be consistent with the incomplete stimulus information. The context may provide sufficient constraints to remove ambiguity about which is the appropriate response. During acquisition, however, the procedures of generation more typically effect a response when the reader has little or no experience of the stimulus word.

In Chapter 4 by Nicholson, in this volume, data are presented in which average progress children younger than eight years showed a positive influence of context on reading accuracy for oral reading of story texts. However, comparable 8-year-olds did not show such an influence of context. (All children were exposed to reading instruction which emphasised reading for meaning.) On the interpretation given by the present theory, the older children had sufficient experience of print words to enable them to use recall procedures for most responses, and hence context would have very little influence as it does not contribute to recall procedures. The younger children with less experience would make more use of generation procedures and hence the influence of context was apparent.

Provided Letter-Sound Correspondences. This source of knowledge would be expected in the experiential history of those readers exposed to explicit phonics instruction. Such instruction is designed to provide information about sounds (phonemes) which are commonly associated with letters. It also attempts to provide information about how the reader may use knowledge of letter-phoneme correspondences to generate a response. (The effects of phonics instruction on processes of reading are considered in Chapter 3 in this volume.) Without phonics instruction this source of knowledge may not be available to the reader, or if available may not be used satisfactorily in generation procedures. It has been argued, however, that (in English) without explicit phonics instruction many letter–phoneme correspondences are also available from the reader's knowledge of the letter names of most consonant letters. For example the /t/ sound is available as the initial sound of the name of the letter 't'. Another argument about children not exposed to phonics instruction is that they will learn elementary letter-sound correspondences by making inferences from their experience of phoneme-to-letter correspondences during the learning of spelling skills. Evidence about both these arguments will be considered in a subsequent section of this chapter.

It must be noted that the provided knowledge of letter–sound correspondences considered here comprises a source which is independent of that given by the learner's induction from print word experience in reading. Hence knowledge of these correspondences will be referred to as 'independent letter–phoneme correspondences'. See Figure 1. There is a range of procedures which use knowledge of independent letter-phoneme correspondences to generate reading responses. At one extreme, only a single letter-phoneme correspondence may be used (usually that for the initial letter(s) of the stimulus) and at the other, phoneme correspondences are determined for all letters of the word. Where more than one phoneme correspondence is determined for a word these phonemes may be combined (assembled) by the reader to form a phonological component or a complete phonological item. Whether it be a single initial phoneme or a complete phonological item, this information is matched, or partially so, against existing words in the learner's (speaking/listening) vocabulary. In the case of the single phoneme the procedure has been called 'cueing' (Ehri, 1987) and in the case of a complete phonological word it could be described as 'sequential decoding' (Marsh *et al.*, 1981; Frith, 1985) with a lexical check. As considered here, these are all instances of the use of the learner's knowledge of independent letter–phoneme correspondences for generation of a reading response. Clearly, with only a single phoneme and hence only a partial match available, there will be many candidate responses (e.g. all words in the learner's spoken vocabulary that begin with /b/). However, other classes of knowledge, namely the sentence context of the stimulus word, and sublexical relations, will contribute information to constrain the candidate responses, in some cases reducing these to a single candidate which becomes the response. Where a complete phonological item is generated but this fails to match any phonological word of the learner's speaking–listening vocabulary a response can still be made. Reading responses to pseudowords (e.g. blof) will be of this kind.

Continuity in Use of Classes of Knowledge for Generation. The use of any one of the three classes of knowledge in generation procedures does not imply a stage or phase for the learner. Mature readers will in some circumstances need to respond to words which they have not previously experienced. On such occasions they will attempt to generate a reading response and may use any one or all of the three classes of knowledge. Usually the learner will use knowledge from all of those sources which are available. The child in the first year of reading instruction will quite frequently be attempting to respond to print words not previously experienced. In doing this, according to the present theory, they will make use of context and sublexical relations to generate a response. If taught to do so, as in explicit phonics instruction, the child is likely to also attempt to use knowledge of independent letter–phoneme correspondences. It should be noted that it is expected that children given phonics instruction will make use of knowledge of sublexical relations as well as of independent letter–phoneme correspondences. According to the present theory, the generation of a response, from whatever classes of knowledge, is not an end point in processing but a means for self-generating associations which are then stored. These are associations between representations of the sequence of letters of the print word and the (lexical) phonological and semantic representations of the word. If the same association is generated at other occurrences of the same print stimulus word (and if these are consistent with any provided associations for the word), then the storage is likely to become sufficiently permanent to enable subsequent activation of recall procedures for the stimulus. See Figure 1.

It is expected that making available a particular source of knowledge will not alter the effectiveness of the contribution of the other sources for generating associations for reading. For example, the availability of context would not reduce the effectiveness of the contribution of knowledge of independent letter–phoneme correspondences to generate associations. Nor would the availability of provided letter–sound correspondences reduce the effectiveness of the contribution of sublexical relations to generate associations for subsequent recall in reading.

Sublexical relations for generation procedures

It remains to elaborate on the nature of the learner's knowledge of sublexical relations for generation procedures, and to present empirical evidence for the learner's knowledge of such, particularly evidence which distinguishes between knowledge of sublexical relations and knowledge of independent letter-phoneme correspondences. This section will describe the nature of sublexical relations in the present theory, and the next section the relevant evidence. Sublexical relations are formed by induction from stored print word experience. This is unlike independent letter–phoneme correspondences which are learnt as separate items of knowledge (e.g. the phoneme /t/ corresponds to the letter 't'), independently of knowledge induced from print word experience.

Sublexical relations are formed between orthographic components and sublexical phonological components. These relations are formed as the child acquires orthographic storage as a consequence of experience with print words. For example, see Figure 2. If the child has learnt to identify the print word 'not', a relation will be formed between the orthographic component 'n-' and the item of the phonological lexicon, /not/. The letter 'n' is represented in the positional context of the left boundary of the orthographic representation of the word. There will also be a relation between /not/ and the orthographic component '-t', where the letter 't' is represented in the positional context of the right boundary of the orthographic representation of the word. The relation between '-o-' and /not/ may be formed later in acquisition. Similarly for 'get', a relation will be formed between 'g-' and /get/ and between '-t' and /get/; and for other lexical contexts, e.g. 'cat', 'went', 'got', not shown in Figure 2. The orthographic component '-t' then has relations with several items of the reader's phonological lexicon, /not/, /get/, /cat/, /went/, and /got/. One phonological component, /-t/, is

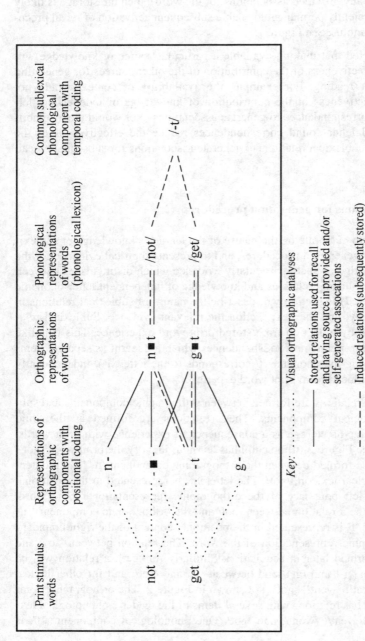

Figure 2 Example of a sublexical relation formed between an orthographic component, 't', and a sublexical phonological component, /-t/.

common to those items. If the child is presented with a previously unlearned print item which includes the orthographic component '-t', then by using relations involving common orthographic and phonological components, the child can induce that '-t' relates to /-t/ when attempting to generate a response to the item. This relation can be used, and often will be, without pronunciation of any segmented components of the word, that is, without 'sounding out'. Similar relations will be formed among all relevant available representations of other orthographic and phonological components in the various positional contexts. Figure 2 shows only a simplification of one sublexical relation in the final position. The sublexical relations are a source of knowledge for generating responses to words when recall procedures are insufficient. The sublexical relations are then used to produce a reading response, being applied in the same range of ways as was described for independent letter–phoneme correspondences. It should be noted, however, that the sublexical relations belong to the internal cognitive processes of the reader. Neither covert nor overt pronunciation ('sounding out') is required, nor is likely to occur.

Sublexical relations among stored information are a source of knowledge for the reader which contributes to generation procedures. These are a means toward the reader's goal of being able to function independently of external teaching assistance. It should be noted that sublexical relations are not sourced directly in experience. They are more abstract, being the learner's induction from the representations of print words previously experienced. See Figure 1. Moreover, sublexical relations are not analogies in the sense that the reader does not select the representations of a known print word, e.g. 'get', and use a component of that, e.g. '-et' as a 'model' for responding to 'et' of the stimulus word 'let'. Sublexical relations are induced between all relevant representations of orthographic components and phonological components which are stored by the reader. They are interlexical categorisations of these components in the various lexical contexts available. Although representations of phonological components are not used for recall they receive activation at the time of recall. This contention is supported by some experimental evidence (Perfetti, Bell & Delany, 1988; Perfetti & Bell, 1991). Activation of phonological components is apparently quite general and occurs very early during recall. This information can then be stored along with information about relevant orthographic components. Such stored information from experience of different lexical contexts is accumulated and categorised to form sublexical relations. As the reader's stored print word experience changes, as more words are added to the learner's orthographic representations, so will the sublexical relations expand. Induction of these relations will be updated continuously by the reader.

Unlike independent letter–phoneme correspondences for which much of the information can be provided through direct teaching, sublexical relations cannot be provided in direct teaching. It would be implausible for the teacher to point out all such relations for each new word as it is acquired. While the large number of these interrelationships is within the capacity of nonconscious processing, the explicit attention to all of them would be overwhelming for both teacher and child. The teacher may, however, use appropriate examples in an attempt to facilitate a generalisable learning strategy involving sublexical relations. Of both theoretical and practical interest is the point of origin, the minimum earliest set of conditions from which a sublexical relation can be formed. This learning sequence is considered next.

Increasing Completeness of Orthographic Representations. There will be a learning sequence in the orthographic representation of words. The learner will not acquire a complete representation of the letters and their order in the word all at once. There may be only representation of one letter and no representation of the relation of that letter to the rest of the print word. With an increasing reading vocabulary, as further discrimination between words is required, some representation is made of the relationship between a component letter and the rest of the print word. For the novice reader the two visual boundaries (left and right) of the print word provide a convenient frame for the parsing and processing involved in the representation of this relationship. A letter which comprises one of these boundaries may be represented and associated with an item of the learner's phonological lexicon. At this point in the learning sequence the identity as either left or right boundary positions may not be represented. Subsequently, the left boundary letter would be represented as such, and later in the learning sequence, the right boundary letter added to the representation, along with some coding which represents the approximate length in number of letters (but not the particular letters) between the word boundaries. This is the point reached for representation of each of the selected words in the example of Figure 2, where left and right boundary letters are represented but not the medial letter (although 3-letter-length is represented). The theoretical terminal state of this learning sequence is complete representation of all letters and their order. It is not necessarily the case that this terminal state is always reached when a word is well known even by the mature reader. In the mature reader when a new word is learnt there will also be a similar learning sequence, although somewhat abbreviated. A computational model of processes by which the increasing completeness of orthographic representation may occur in beginning readers is given in Cassidy (1990).

Alignment with Phonological Components. When this orthographic representation associated with a word has advanced to the point at which a letter receives a representation as belonging to an identified boundary position, say right boundary, it will be possible to make a partial alignment between an orthographic component, e.g. '-t' and a phonological component /-t/ of the word 'not'. See Figure 2. Without such an alignment which matches position of the orthographic component with temporal order of the phonological component, the orthographic component '-t' of 'not' could equally become related with either the phonological component /n-/ or /-t/. Alignment between positional coding of the orthographic component and temporal coding of the phonological component is necessary to avoid such mismatches.

This theoretical account assumes that the learner has access to the identity of segments of phonology as small as the phoneme, e.g. /t/, although the representation would also include information on temporal position of the segment within the phonological representation of the word in which it occurs. With this information a particular phonological component is able to be identified in a particular temporal position of the phonological word, e.g. /t/ in final position, /-t/. See Figure 2. There is much literature pointing to the importance of the learner having access to segments of phonology as small as the phoneme. (See Chapter 6 by Tunmer and Hoover in this volume.) In the present theoretical account, however, emphasis is given to the temporal coding of the segment in relation to the positional coding of orthographic components within words. In the next section empirical evidence will be presented which supports this aspect of the account. It is also an aspect which provides a means for distinguishing between the beginning reader's use of two classes of knowledge in generation procedures: independent letter-phoneme correspondences and sublexical relations. This is one of the main achievements of the empirical studies reported in the next section.

Evidence about sublexical relations

The purpose of this series of experiments was to obtain evidence in the early period of acquisition about the reader's use of sublexical relations formed from stored print word experience. If there are response generation procedures which use this information during the early period of reading acquisition, such use should be most evident when the other information sources for generation are not available, that is, when neither provided letter-sound correspondences nor semantic-syntactic context are available. See Figure 1. There are some previous results (Pick *et al.*, 1978, Study 2) which apparently indicate that in the early period of acquisition the induction of sublexical relations does occur, being manifest under such conditions, but other results (Seymour & Elder, 1986; Bryne & Fielding-Barnsley, 1989, 1990) which show that it does not. There are problems in interpreting all these results. Those in the Pick *et al.* study could have been confounded by including some teaching of spelling of training words, inadvertently providing letter-name and hence some letter–sound correspondences. The

Seymour & Elder study may have failed to detect induced sublexical relations by using transfer criteria comprised of items insufficiently related to the common components likely to be acquired from the reading vocabulary learnt under the natural classroom conditions of the study. Byrne & Fielding-Barnsley included in their training conditions merely single pairs of words with common letter–phoneme relationships. In the present theoretical framework it is not expected that such sparse print word experience would be a sufficient experiential base for the reader's induction of sublexical relations.

The Relationship of Generation Responses to Lexical and Positional Frequency

Formation of a particular sublexical relation depends on the availability of the relevant orthographic and phonological components in the stored representations of words encountered in print. If the relevant components are not in this lexical experience, then the sublexical relations will not be formed. Moreover, as the orthographic components have positional coding, both positional and lexical frequency would be expected to affect the formation of sublexical relations. For example, if the reader has no experience of the letter 't' in the final position of words encountered in print, then the sublexical relation (shown in Figure 2) between the orthographic final 't' component, '-t', and final 't' phoneme, /-t/, will not be formed.

Experiments 1 and 2 (Thompson, Cottrell & Fletcher-Flinn, 1991) were designed to examine the conditions for acquiring sublexical relations. Pseudowords were constructed from graphemes (letter(s) e.g. 'b', 'th', 'ng', corresponding to single phonemes) which varied in lexical and positional frequency in the reading books used in schools. If the child's response generation procedures can use sublexical relations formed from print lexical experience, then lexical and positional frequency of the grapheme components of presented pseudoword items would be expected to affect performance on those items. This influence would be apparent particularly if the child did not use other information sources to generate a response. Response generation procedures are required for pseudowords, as recall is not available for such items which have not been previously experienced. Semantic and syntactic information is of course not available for such stimuli presented as isolated items. In the schools the subjects were not taught letter–sound correspondences as items of knowledge separate from lexical contexts. Hence this source of information would not be expected to have an influence on their performance.

An indication of lexical and positional frequency of orthographic components in the print word experience of the subjects was obtained by a count of the frequency of graphemes in initial and final boundary positions of different words of the texts of books in use for the first year of instruction in schools in

Table 1 Frequency of graphemes in boundary positions among word types* of reading books

	Position	
	Initial	Final
t	85	115
b	141	2

*Total number of types (different words) was 1,575.

the research district. Grapheme 'b' occurred only very rarely in final position but relatively frequently in initial position of words. In contrast, another common consonant grapheme 't' occurred relatively frequently in both final and initial position of words. Table 1 gives the percentage of each of these four orthographic components among word types (the different words or vocabulary) of the 244 reading books used in one large school. A count was also taken of 80 reading books in a smaller school with a smaller resource of books. The results were closely similar. It was expected that the frequency of an orthographic component among word types would give an indication of the number of different lexical contexts for that component which would be available in the child's print word experience. The token frequency (total occurrences) of an orthographic component would be a less useful indicator as very high frequencies may occur but involve only two or three different words.

Initial position components during learning are in general likely to be acquired more quickly than final position components, making performance for initial components better than final where such have the same frequency. However, the present theory about sublexical relations would predict that the children's use of generation procedures for reading would be affected by the differential characteristics of this print word experience, responses for final 'b' being extremely poor relative to final 't'.

In Experiment 1, in order to examine the children's use of generation procedures, pseudowords of two graphemes were constructed, some with 't' in initial position (ta, ti, tu) and others with 't' in final position (et, ot, ut). Similar items were constructed for the letter 'b' (ba, bo, bu and eb, ib, ob). The items were presented for reading, along with filler items, and were grouped by common vowel letter, e.g. ta, ca, ba, ga. Each such block was preceded by a demonstration item, e.g. 'pa' for this block of items, which was pronounced by the experimenter for the child, who was required to imitate the pronunciation.

This was corrected if necessary. These demonstration items provided the child with a pronunciation for the vowel letter which was common to the block of items which followed. All blocks of items with an initial consonant letter either preceded or followed all blocks with a final consonant letter, this order being counterbalanced across subjects. The order of items within each block was randomised individually for each subject.

The subjects in Experiment 1 were 24 English-speaking children aged 5 years 7 months to 6 years 9 months. Reading age scores of the subjects ranged from 5 years 1 month to 6 years 1 month. (New Zealand standardisation of Burt Word Reading Test, extrapolated norms.) As children in New Zealand commence school on their fifth birthday the subjects were in their first year of reading instruction. They were from schools in a suburban area of New Zealand. The book experience approach (Department of Education, 1985) was used by the teachers. This approach emphasises as cues to word identification the semantic–syntactic context of the word and the initial letter of the word (name of letter more commonly than the corresponding sound). Phonics was not taught in so far as the children did not receive systematic classroom instruction in the correspondence between letter sequences and their corresponding sounds, nor instruction in assembly (blending) of sounds. The essentials of this approach to reading instruction has been in use in New Zealand for over 25 years. See the Appendix to this volume for further details.

The subjects' performance for letters 'b' and 't' in pseudowords is shown in Table 2. Correct responses comprised pronunciation of the correct consonant letter and a vowel sound of any kind in the appropriate position. In the case of initial 'b' or 't', a vowel sound of any kind was required to follow the consonant, and in the case of final 'b' or 't' a vowel sound of any kind was required as the preceding initial sound of the child's response. As expected, accuracy for final position 'b' or 't' was lower than for initial position in the pseudowords. However, accuracy was extremely low for final 'b' relative to final 't', although 'b' in initial position produced a performance at least as good as 't' in this position. (Interaction between letters and position was statistically significant at the 0.001 level). Such a differential result for 'b' and 't' in final position is as predicted by the present theory of sublexical relations.

These results of Experiment 1 were very similar to results obtained in Experiment 2 with 24 children of similar age and reading levels in two other schools of the same district using the same teaching approach. In Experiment 2, in addition to 'b' and 't' graphemes, 'm' and 'th' were compared in initial and final position in two-grapheme pseudowords. As with the grapheme 't', 'm' occurs with high frequency in both initial and final position among word types (vocabulary) but 'th' occurs infrequently in final position. The results in

Table 2 Mean percentage of correct responses to letters in each position of pseudowords: Experiment 1

	Position	
	Initial	*Final*
t	71	56
b	86	17

Experiment 2 for 'th' and 'm' reflected this lexical and positional frequency in the same way as the results for 'b' and 't'. Performance for 'b' and 'th' relative to 't' and 'm' was lower in final position to a greater extent than in initial position. (Interaction between position and graphemes 'b' & 'th' versus 't' & 'm' was statistically significant at the 0.05 level).

These two sets of results match the predictions from the present theory about the learner's induction from print word experience of sublexical relations between orthographic and phonological components. However, it remains to clarify whether or not the present results could be attributed to the learner's use of any knowledge of independent letter–phoneme correspondences in generation procedures for reading. If the subjects did have this knowledge for the letter 't' but not for 'b' this would explain the poor final 'b' performance (Table 2) but would fail to explain why their performance for 'b' in initial position is as good as that for 't' in initial position. It would also fail to explain other data in Experiment 2. The letters were also presented in isolation and subjects were required to provide a sound for each. Accuracy for 'b' was 90% and that for 't', 92%.

Alternatively, it may be argued that the subjects have knowledge of independent letter–phoneme correspondences for both 'b' and 't' but somehow have extreme difficulty applying this knowledge to 'b' in final position but not to 't' in this position. The problem with this explanation is that it gives no reason why such difficulty should apply to 'b' much more than 't'. There is then no reason on these grounds to reject the interpretation of the data as matching the predictions.

Nevertheless, the data are a set of associations only. The word count frequency in these associations also indicates frequency of pronunciation of the words as well as frequency of print experience. The child's experience of these pronunciations could be producing the observed associations as much as any experience of the print words. The frequency of exposure to print words has not been directly manipulated, for example, by providing experience of words with final 'b'. Convergent results from such an experimental manipulation would strengthen the interpretation given. Experiment 3 was designed to make this manipulation and control for experience of word pronunciation by examining it both with and without print word experience.

Manipulation of the Learner's Print Lexicon

The purpose of this experiment (Thompson, Cottrell & Fletcher-Flinn, 1991) was to control the learners' experience of words from which they could induce a sublexical relation, in this case the relation between the final 'b' orthographic component and final /b/ phonological component. Subjects were selected who showed negligible use of final 'b' sublexical relations in the generation procedures required for pseudowords with final 'b'. The subjects were provided with print experience of target words containing the final 'b' orthographic component, and then retested for evidence of their induction of the sublexical relation from that print word experience. Such evidence would comprise increased use of final 'b' sublexical relations in generation procedures of reading.

Twelve children were selected from those in Experiment 1, each showing near negligible accuracy (5%) on final 'b' (in pseudowords ab, ob, eb, ib, ub) but high accuracy (83%) on initial 'b' (in pseudowords ba, bo, bu). (Final 't' was 53% and initial 't' 72%.) In addition they had near negligible accuracy on a pretest of the target print words with final 'b' (3%). The subjects were randomly assigned to an experimental (seven subjects) and a control condition (five subjects). The experimental group received both print and reading pronunciation experience of the target words. The control group received pronunciation experience without print experience of the words. Over a period of two weeks the experimental subjects were provided with individual instruction that included reading of the eight target words with final 'b', crab, grab, cab, jab, job, rob, bob, mob. Each of these words was embedded in a simple sentence, e.g. 'It is my job to feed the cat'. Eight such sentences were constructed for each target word (with a balanced variation in the position of the target word in the sentences). These 64 sentences formed a pool from which sentences were selected for each learning trial. This comprised the child's oral reading of a sentence with correction by the experimenter of all reading errors and omissions. The child was required to pronounce each such correction (as a complete word). No sound components of words were provided for the children and they did not produce segmented sounds except occasionally for the initial letter of a word. For each target word there were 20 learning trials, two on each of four days in the first week and four on each of three days in the second week. Four days following the last learning trial the pseudoword test and test of target words were repeated.

Table 3 Effect of learning to read words with final 'b': Experiment 3

	Experimental	*Control*
Mean increment in percentage correct reading of training words with final 'b'	+78%	+8%
Transfer to pseudowords: Mean increment in percentage correct readings of final 'b' in pseudowords	+29%	0%
Mean reading age (years and months)	5–8	5–8
Mean picture vocabulary standard score	100	104

The control subjects received the same sentences over the same number of trials but with the target word and one other word deleted from each printed sentence. The children in the control group read these sentences and the experimenter supplied the pronunciation for the deleted words. The child imitated these pronunciations. Corrections were provided for the children's reading errors. Control subjects received the same pretests and post-tests as the experimental subjects.

The main results are given in Table 3. In reading the target training words the experimental subjects made an extremely large performance increment from pretest to the (retention) post-test; while the control subjects showed an almost negligible increment. The transfer to performance on final 'b' of the pseudowords was large and positive as shown by the pre- to post-test increment for the experimental subjects. Six of the seven experimental subjects showed a positive increment. There was a zero increment for every one of the control subjects. (The statistical difference between experimental and control subjects was significant at the 0.01 level. Moreover, there was not a statistically significant increment in performance on initial 'b', initial or final 't'; nor any significant differences between the experimental and control subjects in such increments.)

The results of Experiment 3 are consistent with the theoretical prediction that as a consequence of experience of print words with a final 'b' orthographic component, the experimental subjects were able to induce the sublexical relation between the final 'b' orthographic component and final 'b' phonological component, and use this relation in generation procedures for responses to the pseudowords at the time of the post-test. The results cannot be explained by ascribing them to the learner's use of knowledge of independent letter–phoneme correspondences. The experimental learning sessions did not provide any direct instruction in letter–sound correspondences within words. Moreover, if unknown to the investigators, such teaching did occur in the classrooms between pretest and post-test, it would have affected the responses of the subjects in the control condition as much as the experimental condition, as both were from the same classrooms and the teachers did not know which children were experimental and which were control subjects.

By the theoretical account given here it was supposed that in this experiment the learner has formed a sublexical relation to a component as small as the phoneme segment, namely /b/. It is important to consider whether the results in this experiment are consistent with this account or whether they would better fit an alternative view that learners in this early period of acquisition are using only larger phonological segments, for example segments such as 'rimes', e.g. /-æb/ of /kræb/ for the word 'crab'. Half of the target words in the experimental condition had '-ab' rimes and half had '-ob' rimes. If the subjects were forming relations with a coding of these rime segments, then it would be expected that their correct responses to the pseudowords would show greater increments for those pseudowords which were rimes of the target training words, namely 'ab' and 'ob'. Such was not the case. The increments in percentage accuracy for the final 'b' pseudowords were as follows: ab 0%, ob 70%, eb 15%, ib 45%, ub 15%. (The mean increment in percentage correct reading of the target words ending in '-ab' was 78% and for those ending in '-ob' also 78%).

In summary, the evidence obtained shows that very young learners can use sublexical relations in generation procedures for reading, and that this class of knowledge is distinct from knowledge of independent letter–phoneme correspondences such as may be acquired from phonics instruction. From quite limited stored print word experience the learners induced sublexical relations between orthographic and phonological components. These relations were a source of knowledge in the learner's generation procedures for reading. The phonological components were segments as small as the phoneme. They were also specific to temporal position of the component in relation to position of the orthographic component within the word, in a way which cannot be explained by the use of independent letter–phoneme correspondences. Hence, sublexical relations were used as a source of knowledge in generation for reading when the learners did not use knowledge of independent letter-phoneme correspondences.

It may be added that Experiment 3 has also been conducted with children of eight years having severe reading disability. The children were matched on

reading age to those in Experiment 3. Most failed to acquire the sublexical relation, even though they were more successful than the normal reading age
matched children in knowledge of the critical independent letter-phoneme correspondence (Fletcher-Flinn, Thompson & Cottrell, 1992).

The evidence in relation to other theories

In the present theory sublexical relations are induced from stored representations of experiences of print words (see Figure 1). Such is not the case in theories of acquisition which accept the 'bypass hypothesis' (Van Orden et al.,
1990). This hypothesis states that children early in their learning respond to
words by using knowledge of independent letter–phoneme correspondences and
then subsequently bypass this phonological mediation to form direct connections
between the orthographic representation and the meaning(s) of the word. There
is nothing in this hypothesis to account for generation procedures based on
knowledge gained from print word experience. There is nothing to explain the
results of Experiment 3.

The bypass hypothesis, in various versions, is a part of the several developmental theories that postulate successive phases of development (Marsh et
al., 1981; Frith, 1985; Seymour, 1990). In these there is a phase in which the
mature reader can bypass previously acquired phonological mediation by direct
connections between the representation of the letters of the word and the mean-
ing(s) of the word. A modification of this developmental phase theory has been
proposed by Jorm & Share (1983). They claimed that the empirical evidence is
better explained by postulating a continuous change in which direct connections (recall) become more probable than generation procedures as the experience of the learner increases. This would be consistent with the present theory
if, for the beginning reader, generation procedures included sublexical relations
but in Jorm & Share's account this was not the case. Jorm & Share (p. 114)
did consider the possibility that the beginning reader may carry out generation
of reading responses by procedures involving the use of orthographic neigh-
bours (Glushko, 1979), e.g. words with common components, 'crab', 'cab',
'jab'. Unlike independent letter–phoneme correspondences such procedures use
knowledge from stored representations of print words for which direct connections have already been acquired. Jorm & Share rejected this possibility. Hence
in their theory phonological mediation for the beginning reader did not extend
beyond letter–phoneme correspondences, the source of which was independent
of stored representations of acquired print words. The results of Experiment 3
were not consistent with this view. Beginning readers were able to make use of
experience of a small number of print words to induce sublexical relations

which provided an alternative procedure for achieving phonological mediation.

Another alternative generation procedure which has been proposed is the formation of analogies with print words already acquired. Goswami & Bryant (1990) claim that beginning readers make such analogies using 'rime' segments of acquired words. Evidence for their claim is quite limited in so far as it is restricted to the influence of such analogies in short term effects and has not included the longer-term effects of retention required as learning takes place. In describing the results of Experiment 3 it has already been observed that they are inconsistent with this analogy procedure of phonological mediation. Further experiments are being conducted by our research group to determine whether beginning readers are advantaged for learning a word like 'rug' when they have had prior experience of words with the same rime unit (e.g. jug, bug, tug). Preliminary results from learning trials conducted over periods of three weeks show no learning advantage. This is in spite of the fact that substitution errors indicate that readers give more attention to the medial vowel letter than in the control condition where the words, though having common vowels, do not have common rime units. These preliminary results indicate that while learners are sensitive to common units larger than a single letter such units are not useful in mediating retention for learning.

Ehri (1992) has offered an alternative to the bypass hypothesis. She has proposed that the reader initially responds with independent letter–phoneme correspondences. However these are not bypassed but on repeated use with a particular print word the correspondences become established in a word-specific 'visual–phonologic' representation. This includes connections between individual letters and individual phonemes of the particular word. The 'visual–phonologic' representation is used for recall of the word. However, there is nothing in Ehri's theoretical account to indicate that this 'visual–phonologic' representation is usable for generation procedures, as are the sublexical relations of the present theory. Without any such generation procedures, Ehri's account cannot explain the results of Experiments 1 and 2. These indicate that the child (without explicit phonics instruction) is unlikely to generate an accurate response to a letter in final position of a novel (pseudoword) item if the child has had little print word experience of the letter in that position. Nor can the account explain the results of Experiment 3 which demonstrate how such print word experience does affect generation procedures through sublexical relations.

In another quite different theoretical approach Seidenberg & McClelland (1989) have constructed a computational model of subsymbolic connections between orthography and phonology. While Seidenberg & McClelland address the question of the acquisition of reading skill, they do not attempt to fit the model to any early acquisition data in their reported work. Nevertheless, their model exemplifies an important theoretical concept: the same domain of connections can provide responses both for recall of learnt words and for generation of responses to words not previously seen. The particular nature of these connections in their model entails that relationships between adjacent letters of print words would be acquired by the learner and these relationships would be involved in the learner's attempts to generate responses to words or pseudowords. In Experiment 3 beginning readers did not consistently use relationships between adjacent letters of known print words (e.g. 'ab' of crab, grab, cab, jab) to achieve a response for pseudowords composed of such adjacent letters. In this respect the results of Experiment 3 are inconsistent with the Seidenberg & McClelland model.

The last theoretical alternative to be considered is the notion of 'logographic' reading. This is reading based on the association between meaning of the word and visual features of the print word, where those features do not include the alphabetic letters. In the theory of Frith (1985) a phase of 'logographic' reading is postulated as the earliest phase of acquisition, preceding the use of letter-phoneme correspondences. The 5- and 6-year-old children in Experiments 1 to 3 were not 'logographic' readers. To make the sublexical relations which they achieved it is clear that representation of some alphabetic letters of words was required. These results, however, do not contradict the evidence (Ehri & Wilce, 1985) that children may employ 'logographic' reading at an earlier level of learning when print word experience is minimal.

Evidence about other sources of knowledge

There are accounts of reading acquisition which propose other sources of knowledge for generation procedures, in particular through transfer from existing skills. In the present theory these sources are not included as contributing to generation procedures. See Figure 1. The reasons for not including them are presented in this section. It has been claimed that the learner acquires knowledge of particular phoneme-to-letter correspondences in spelling and that this knowledge transfers as a source of knowledge for particular letter-phoneme correspondences used in generation procedures for reading (Frith, 1985; Seymour & MacGregor, 1984). The evidence about this for beginning readers is quite limited. The comparisons made by Bryant & Bradley (1980) and Bradley & Bryant (1979) were of word reading and word spelling. No attempt was made to compare the knowledge of particular letter–phoneme with phoneme-to-letter correspondences, without confounding this with the subjects' knowledge of specific print words. Nevertheless, the claim, if true, has important implications for teaching practice in so far as knowledge of letter–phoneme correspondences could be acquired from the child's spelling experience, without being provided for the child by more direct teaching, as occurs with explicit phonics instruction. Stuart & Coltheart (1988) have made a somewhat different proposal, but it also includes the claim that knowledge for generation of reading responses can have its source in the child's experience of phoneme-to-letter correspondences. Another claim is that letter names provide a source (in some cases inconsistent) for knowledge of particular letter-phoneme correspondences in generation procedures for reading (Venezky, 1975; Mason, 1984). Empirical evidence will be presented concerning each of these claims. The purpose of Experiments 4 and 5 was to examine the claim that letter names provide a source of knowledge for generation procedures. The claim about spelling experience as a similar source will be examined subsequently.

Letter Names

The rationale of Experiment 4 (Thompson, Fletcher-Flinn & Cottrell, 1991) is that if letter names have been the source of the beginning reader's knowledge of particular letter–phoneme correspondences in generation procedures for reading, then their knowledge of correspondences will be highly inaccurate where letter names provide misleading information about corresponding sounds of letters. In English the letter names for 'c' and 'g' are especially clear examples. The initial sound of the letter name for 'c' is /s/ rather than /k/, and the initial sound for 'g' is /dz/ (initial sound of *jam*) rather than /g/. In this experiment the letters 'c' and 'g' were presented (along with other letters) and the subjects asked to provide the sound for each. On a subsequent day they were presented with two-letter pseudowords, some of which contained 'c' and 'g' in initial position (ca, co, cu and ga, gi, gu) and others in final position (ac, ec, oc and ag, ig, ug). The subjects were the same as in Experiment 1. They were beginning readers who had not received explicit phonics instruction. The items were presented along with those of Experiment 1, the order of presentation blocked and counterbalanced in the same way. The scoring of responses to the initial and final letters took the same form.

The results are given in Table 4. The accuracy of reading responses for 'c' and 'g' was higher when in initial position of a pseudoword and very low when presented as an isolated letter. (The difference between the accuracy for the initial position and isolated conditions was statistically significant at the 0.001 level). For the isolated letters there was a high percentage of substitution error responses, which was as expected if letter names were the source of knowledge. The sound /s/ was given for the letter 'c' and /dz/ for the letter 'g'. However, the percentage of such substitution errors was low for these letters in initial position of a pseudoword. (The difference between the initial position

Table 4 Phoneme correspondence responses to letters c and g: Experiment 4

| | | | Position in pseudoword | |
		Isolated	Initial	Final
Mean	c	28	51	24
percentage				
correct	g	18	50	18
Mean	c → /s/	58	24	3
percentage*				
substitution	g → /dz/	68	33	7
errors				

* Percentage of total responses

and isolated conditions was statistically significant at the 0.001 level). This is in contrast to the results for 'b' and 't' with the same subjects (Experiment 1) in which accuracy of responses to these letters was very high, both in initial position of the pseudowords and when presented in isolation.

The hypothesis that letter names are a source for letter–phoneme correspondence knowledge used in generation procedures can explain these results for the letters presented in isolation but it fails to explain the results for the letters 'c' and 'g' when in the initial position of pseudowords. Here at least half of the subjects in generating a reading response do not use any such letter–phoneme correspondence knowledge they may have derived from letter names. Alternatively, the learner's use of sublexical relations would explain the results for pseudowords. The count of frequency of graphemes in initial and final position of words in the texts of reading books, used in the schools of the district, showed that 90 different words appeared which contained an initial 'c' grapheme (98% corresponding to the phoneme /k/) and only 4 with 'c' in final position (e.g. 'music'). There were 61 with an initial 'g' grapheme (93% corresponding to the phoneme /g/) and 16 with a 'g' grapheme in final position. A count from a second sample of books gave similar results. Thus there was ample opportunity from their print word experience for the subjects to acquire the sublexical relations c : /k/ and g : /g/ for initial position but very restricted opportunity for final position. (Accuracy of responses to final position letters was very low. See Table 4.)

So these readers, who have been taught without explicit phonics instruction, when presented with a novel word are likely to generate a response for the initial letter from sublexical relations, and when presented with an isolated consonant letter respond with a sound that derives from the letter name. Before leaving this as a conclusion, another possible interpretation will be examined. It could be possible that the readers' response to the letters in isolation derived not directly from their knowledge of letter names but through their knowledge of phoneme-to-letter correspondences in spelling. Such correspondences in the learner's spelling knowledge have been claimed to sometimes derive from letter name knowledge (Read, 1986). So if the sounds that beginning readers give in response to isolated letters are derived in this indirect way through spelling, then it would be expected that the phoneme /s/ would be spelt by beginning readers as the letter 'c' at least as frequently as /s/ is given, in generation for reading, as the phoneme corresponding to 'c' presented in isolation; and similarly for /dz/ and 'g'. This alternative hypothesis was tested in Experiment 5 (Thompson, Fletcher-Flinn & Cottrell, 1991).

In the 'spelling' condition of Experiment 5 the sounds /s/ and /dz/, each with a minimal following schwa vowel sound, were presented three times, among filler items. Subjects were required to select a letter to match the sound, from a randomised array of 14 letters. In the 'reading' condition the subject was presented with the isolated letters 'c' and 'g' (among others) and required to make a pronunciation for each. The two conditions were presented with the order counterbalanced over subjects and a lapse of at least six days between conditions. The subjects were 13 English-speaking 5-year-olds drawn from two schools. They had not participated in the previous experiments but had received the same type of reading instruction. Their reading attainment was at a similar level to that of the subjects in Experiment 4. The results contradicted the alternative spelling knowledge hypothesis. The phoneme /s/ was spelt as the letter 'c' *less* frequently than was /s/ given as the reading response for the isolated letter 'c'. The result was similar for /dz/ and 'g'. (The overall difference in these substitutions, between the spelling and reading conditions, was statistically significant at the 0.02 level.)

Hence the conclusion can stand that the beginning reader who has not received phonics instruction responds to *isolated* letters with a sound that directly derives from the letter name. However, when responding to a novel word rather than an isolated letter, the same readers are unlikely to use sounds from letter names as a source of knowledge for generating a reading response. They are likely to generate a response from sublexical relations derived from their experience of print words. They do not apply letter–phoneme correspondences derived from their knowledge of letter names. The results are not consistent with the claim that letter names are a source of knowledge for generation procedures for word reading in children with some print experience. On the other hand, the results do not contradict the claim (Scott & Ehri, 1990) that knowledge of letter names facilitates word reading responses of children at an earlier level of learning for whom print experience is minimal. Nor do the results contradict the possibility that knowledge of letter names at the very early level would facilitate the learner's access to phoneme segments and their identities (which are required to form sublexical relations). These would be very early general effects, not particular correspondences which are the topic of concern here.

Phoneme-to-letter Correspondences of Spelling

The other claim is that phoneme-to-letter correspondences acquired in spelling are a source of the reader's letter-phoneme correspondence knowledge used in generation procedures for reading. The implications of the claim for interpreting the findings of Experiments 1 and 2 will be considered. In these experiments the failure of learners to make use of particular letter-phoneme correspondences in generation procedures could be explained by a lack of knowledge of the relevant phoneme-to-letter correspondences in spelling. This explanation was able to be tested as data about the readers' knowledge of phoneme-to-letter correspondences were obtained in Experiment 2 (Thompson, Cottrell & Fletcher-Flinn, 1991).

In addition to the reading condition, in Experiment 2 there was also a 'spelling' condition. In this the pseudowords were presented in auditory form, e.g. /ob/. Each subject was required to pronounce this sound, then select a letter to complete a print display, e.g. o_ , where the correct response is selection of the letter 'b'. The subject's pronunciation was corrected by the experimenter if necessary. Demonstration items were presented and paralleled those in the reading condition. The two conditions were presented with the order counterbalanced over subjects and a lapse of at least three days between conditions.

Accuracy for phoneme-to-letter correspondences in the 'spelling' condition was high, averaging 80% over the phonemes /t/, /m/, /b/ and /th/ in initial and final positions. Unlike the reading condition, the phoneme-to-letter correspondences did not show a significant overall position effect nor was there significant variation between the four phonemes in the extent of any such position effects. The learners' knowledge of phoneme-to-letter correspondences does not explain their particular failures in using generation procedures for reading. For example, in the reading condition they had very low accuracy (26%) in giving a pronunciation for the letter b in final position of pseudowords but were much more accurate (49%) for 't' in final position. Their phoneme-to-letter accuracy in the 'spelling' condition was uniformly high for both /b/ (82%) and /t/ (79%) in final position.

Experiment 6 (Thompson, Fletcher-Flinn & Cottrell, 1991) was conducted to further examine discrepancies between knowledge of phoneme-to-letter correspondences and parallel letter-phoneme correspondences. The motivation was to determine whether knowledge of phoneme-to-letter correspondences was at least as good as knowledge of the parallel letter–phoneme correspondences, as would be expected by the claim that phoneme-to-letter correspondences used in spelling are a source of the reader's knowledge of letter–phoneme correspondences in generation procedures for reading. The kind of letter–phoneme correspondences so far considered are context free in so far as the correspondence holds irrespective of the grapheme context (the letters which precede or follow the grapheme component). For example, /b/ is the phoneme corresponding to grapheme 'b' in any grapheme context of an English morpheme. (Note that 'lamb' is not an exception here as 'mb', not 'b', is the final grapheme of this word.) There are, however, more complex letter-phoneme correspondences which are contingent on variations in grapheme context. For example, in New Zealand English /i:/ (vowel sound of *we*) is the phoneme corresponding to the final grapheme 'y' of 'baby', 'happy' etc., whereas /aɪ/ (vowel sound of *pipe*) is the phoneme that corresponds to the grapheme 'y' in 'my', 'fly', etc. In Experiment 6 the young readers' knowledge of these two context-contingent classes for the phoneme correspondence of the final position grapheme 'y' was examined, along with the class of cases in which the letter 'y' is a component of the grapheme 'ay' in final position, e.g. as in 'day', 'play'. In none of these three cases is the phoneme for 'y' the same as for 'y' in the initial position of words. The young readers' knowledge of these three final position grapheme–phoneme correspondences was compared with their knowledge of the parallel phoneme-to-grapheme correspondences.

The readers would be expected to be at least as proficient in knowledge of the phoneme-to-grapheme correspondences as the parallel grapheme-phoneme correspondences if the experiment were to support the claim that phoneme-to-grapheme correspondences used in spelling are a source of grapheme–phoneme correspondences used in generation procedures for reading. The alternative claim that letter names provide a source of letter–phoneme correspondence knowledge cannot explain these two context-contingent cases. The letter name for 'y' could only provide the consonantal /w/ sound. Another alternative expectation, from the present theory, is that where letter–phoneme correspondences do not have a source in provided correspondences, as from phonics instruction, then sublexical relations induced from the reader's experience of print words will be a sufficient source of knowledge. To obtain information on this alternative, the readers' knowledge of reading and spelling of final 'y' and 'ay' graphemes in real words was tested in order to obtain an indication of any successful print word experience, and spelling experience, the readers had of these graphemes in print lexical contexts. The subjects' knowledge of grapheme–phoneme and phoneme-to-grapheme correspondences was tested in pseudowords so that there was not a confounding with their word-specific knowledge.

In the 'reading' condition eight real word exemplars of each of the classes of words were presented for reading (baby, happy, ...; my, fly, ...; day, play, ...). Unrelated filler words were included among the presented items. Parallel pseudowords were constructed and presented for reading in another test session (goky, feny, tivy, muzy; ky, fy, vy, zy; tay, nay, vay, zay). Demonstration items were provided. No correction was given for errors on any experimental items. The sessions were at least a week apart. The subjects were 27 English-speaking children aged 5 years 4 months to 6 years 10 months (mean 6 years 4 months). They were drawn from the same two schools as the subjects in Experiment 3. Their instruction did not include explicit phonics. They had reading ages on the New Zealand standardised word reading test of 6 years 3 months to 7 years 1 month (mean 6 years 7 months). The mean spelling age was 6 years 3 months (English standardisation, Vernon, 1977) and the mean standard score on the British Picture Vocabulary Scale was 102.

The results for correct responses to the final grapheme of each item are shown in Table 5. For example, the correct response to the final grapheme of 'goky' is /iː/ (vowel sound of *we*). In 'reading' half or more of the subjects gave correct responses for the final grapheme in each class of real words, and also pseudowords except for the 'ky' class. An item analysis showed that these results were consistent over items.

In the 'spelling completion' condition items were presented in auditory form, e.g. /beɪbiː/ (spoken sound of *baby*). The subject was required to pro- nounce the item and then select a grapheme to complete a print display, e.g. bab_ , where the correct response is selection of the grapheme 'y'. The sub- ject's pronunciation was corrected if necessary. The subjects selected respons- es from an array of 10 graphemes (y, a, e, i, o, ay, ai, ea, ee, oo). The order of graphemes in the array was randomised for each subject. Demonstration items were provided and unrelated filler items included. The real word items were presented in one session and the pseudowords in another at least a week apart. The pseudoword spelling completion and pseudoword reading conditions were presented with the order counterbalanced over subjects and a lapse of at least a week between conditions.

More than half the subjects gave correct spelling completion responses to each class of real words but accuracy was very low for the pseudowords. See Table 5. Only spelling completion responses to the 'goky' class of items were significantly above the random response level of 10% (0.01 significance level

Table 5 Mean percentage of correct responses to classes of words and pseudowords: Experiment 6

Exemplars of each class:	baby goky	my ky	day tay
Phoneme for final position grapheme (Reading)			
Words	56	56	81
Pseudowords	48	30	50
Grapheme for final position phoneme (Spelling completion)			
Words	65	59	72
Pseudowords	23	7	18

for the 'goky' class). An item analysis showed that the results were consistent across items.

In these classes of grapheme context-contingent correspondences the accuracy in knowledge of phoneme-to-grapheme correspondences used in spelling completion is clearly lower than accuracy of grapheme-phoneme correspondences in reading, in spite of the fact that accuracy for both spelling and reading of real words is relatively high. Hence the results are inconsistent with the claim that phoneme-to-letter correspondences used in spelling are a source for the beginning reader's knowledge of letter–phoneme correspondences used in generation procedures for reading.

By the alternative account, from the present theory, it is expected that sublexical relations induced from the reader's experience of print words would suffice for generating a reading response to the pseudowords. In this theoretical account boundary letters receive priority for representation in the learning sequence. Hence it would be expected that young readers would be able to induce sublexical relations between final 'y' or 'ay' graphemes and the corresponding phonological components of words containing them that have entered their print word experience. However, in addition there is the context-contingent characteristic which makes it necessary to distinguish the corresponding phoneme, /i:/, for the final 'y' of 'goky' from the phoneme /aɪ/ for the final y of 'ky'. This distinction can be made in the elementary representation of letter length of words, which in the present theory also has priority for representation in the learning sequence. Items of the 'goky' class have greater letter length than those of the 'ky' class.

Half the subjects showed that they had made the correct grapheme–phoneme correspondence for final 'y' of items in the 'goky' class but far fewer were correct on items of the 'ky' class. Nevertheless, in responding to the final 'y' of the 'ky' class of items /i:/ was given as a response with a frequency of only 20%. Hence some discrimination had been made. If it had not been, then the /i:/ response to final 'y' of 'ky' type items would be expected to be as frequent as to 'goky' items, at 48%. Responses to 'ky' type items were at a much lower level of accuracy than responses to 'goky' type items, probably because the subjects had received much less print experience of the 'my' class of words than the 'baby' class. In the count (made for Experiments 1 and 2) of words in one sample of reading books there were 82 different words of the 'baby' class, i.e. with the final y : /i:/ correspondence; only 8 of the 'my' class, i.e. with the final y: /aɪ/ correspondence; and 22 of the 'day' class. Similar differences were apparent in the count of word types from the second sample of books. The results for these context-contingent letter-phoneme correspondences are consistent with the explanation from the present theoretical account. The responses are generated from position-specific sublexical relations induced from the reader's experience of print words.

To summarise, while young learners have knowledge of context-contingent letter-phoneme correspondences such as those for the final 'y' graphemes, they have almost no knowledge of the parallel context-contingent phoneme-to-letter correspondences of spelling. However, young learners who are competent at making some letter–phoneme correspondences, such as for initial 'b', fail on others, such as 'b' in final position, but they are very competent at the parallel phoneme-to-letter correspondences in both positions (Experiment 2). These results do not support the claim that particular phoneme-to-letter correspondences, used in spelling, function as sources of knowledge of particular letter–sound correspondences for generation procedures by beginning readers not exposed to phonics instruction. This conclusion, however, does not contradict the possibility that experience of spelling will at a very early learning level facilitate the learner's access to phoneme segments and their identities (which are required for formation of sublexical relations and for use of independent letter-phoneme correspondences). These would be very early effects and general rather than specific to particular correspondences. There remain three sources of knowledge which contribute directly to generation procedures: (a) Sublexical relations induced from print word experience, (b) Provided letter-sound correspondences where these are available as in phonics instruction, and (c) Semantic and syntactic context. See Figure 1. In the next section consideration is given to the relationships between the contributions of knowledge from these sources.

Relationships between contributions of knowledge from different sources

Semantic and syntactic context of the print word can contribute as a source of knowledge for generation procedures but not involve knowledge of orthographic components nor relations between orthographic and phonological components of the word. This knowledge is thereby different from that of the other two sources: provided letter–sound correspondences, and print word experience from which sublexical relations are formed. (See Figure 1.) It may therefore be argued that as context does not directly engage orthographic components its use, even where correct associations are generated, will result in a poor quality of association for subsequent retention and recall. This would be expected, in so far as those classes of the reader's knowledge which do engage orthographic components contribute less to generation procedures when context is available. This would involve a compensatory relationship between the contributions of the different classes of knowledge to generation procedures. On the other hand, the relationship between the contributions may not be compensatory but independent and parallel, the availability of context in no way reducing the extent of the contribution of the other classes of knowledge. It was the purpose of Experiments 7 and 8 to obtain evidence to distinguish between these theoretical alternatives.

The quality of associations generated was assessed in these experiments by the level of retention of responses to words following training trials conducted either under a low context or a high context condition. As evidence will be given that there were at least as many correctly generated associations under the high as the low context condition, any reduction in the quality of *correctly* generated associations when context is available would be apparent if there were lower overall retention of responses under training with context than without. In addition to retention of word reading responses, retention of particular orthographic components of the words was determined. To avoid confounding the effects of correctly and incorrectly generated responses, correction was provided by the experimenter for all responses made in the training trials.

Most studies which have examined the quality of learning of print words under variations in availability of context have compared training trials with words presented in sentences and words presented in isolation. Although largely avoided in one study (Ehri & Roberts, 1979), a major problem in interpreting such comparisons is that they involve both the pre-identification and post-identification influences of contexts of the words. In the present question the concern is with the pre-identification influence of context, that is the semantic and syntactic context available to contribute to identification of the word, through generation procedures. A meaningful sentence may not only provide this pre-identification context but also provide context which enables the reader to assign a specific meaning to a word which if identified in isolation may be given another meaning, if any at all. This second kind of influence of context, providing disambiguation and instantiation, functions after the word has been identified. For example, the word 'pattern' may designate a cutting guide as for dressmaking or designate a decorative visual design. The sentence 'The pattern was painted by that artist' provides a context supplying a particular meaning for the word 'pattern'. The sentence context provides this for any reader comprehending the sentence, whether or not it has provided pre-identification context for the word. This post-identification context can plausibly influence retention of responses to the print words but of course it is not available for a word presented in isolation.

As the intention in these experiments was to manipulate pre-identification context during reading training with as little confounding as possible with the disambiguation and instantiation effects of context, words were presented in sentences only, but in the 'low context' condition the word appeared as the second word of a meaningful sentence (e.g. 'The pattern was painted for Mother') and in the 'high context' condition it was at or near the end of the sentence (e.g. 'The girl is painting a pattern'). A pool of 60 regularly spelt two syllable target words (pattern, wagon, carpet, etc.) was used and a matching pair of sentences constructed for each, for the high and the low context conditions. Experiment 7 was conducted with each subject over four successive days. On the first day the $6^1/_2$-year-old subjects were given a word reading pretest of the complete pool of target words. For each subject 40 target words were randomly selected from among those of the pool for which the subject failed to give a correct reading response. Then for each subject half the 40 target words were randomly assigned to a training set and the other half to a control set. On the following day subjects attempted oral reading of the sentences, either low or high context, constructed for the 20 words in the training set. This set of 20 sentences was presented twice, in random orders, in the same session. All reading errors were corrected by the experimenter after providing at least three seconds for the child to respond to each word. On the third day one further trial of the training sentences was given. Control words were not presented at all during training. On the fourth day a retention test of both training and control words was conducted.

In this test both training and control words were presented as isolated words. In order to determine retention of specific orthographic components as well as word responses, there were three conditions of presentation of the training and control words in this retention test. In two of these conditions a spelling completion test of the words was conducted as well as the word reading test. The subjects were assigned at random to each condition, with six subjects for each of the six conditions (three test conditions × two context conditions). In the retention test of word reading the conditions varied the completeness of presentation of the print word: (a) complete print word, e.g. 'pattern', (b) word with first vowel letter missing, e.g. p ttern, (c) with second vowel letter missing, e.g. patt rn. Subjects in conditions (b) and (c) of the retention test, immediately after attempting to read each incomplete word (no correction being given), were required to make a spelling completion response by selecting a single vowel letter, a, e, i, o or u, to complete the spelling of the word. The words were such that absence of either vowel allowed not more than one correct identification response. The subjects had reading ages of 6 years 5 months to 7 years 5 months. They were drawn from five schools and had experienced the same kind of reading instruction as the subjects in the previous experiments.

In all three training trials accuracy of reading attempts for training words was much higher (24%, 69%, 80%) under the high than the low context training condition (8%, 46%, 60%). On the retention word reading test there was not a significant difference between high and low context training conditions in the extent to which accuracy of reading responses to training words exceeded control words. This was the case for all three test conditions. Over the three test conditions, the training-control *difference* in percentage accuracy of word reading was 20 percentage points for high context and 24 percentage points for low context. (The percentage accuracy for control words was respectively 8% and 10%.) There was a similar result for spelling completion of first vowel letters. The level of performance for second vowel letters was not significantly above chance.

The results indicate that during the training trials the subjects were making more use of context in the high than the low context condition. However, this difference did not result in any retention difference. Hence the evidence from this experiment does not support the proposition that there is a compensatory relationship between the contributions of context and the other classes of knowledge for generation procedures. The greater availability of pre-identification context did not result in poorer quality of correct associations for subsequent retention. However, the word reading results for retention in this experiment were at a low level of accuracy, little more than 30%.

A second experiment was conducted to obtain evidence on the same question but at higher levels of overall accuracy, with older readers. The 48 subjects in Experiment 8 were aged 8 years and had reading age levels of 7 years 7 months to 8 years 11 months. They were drawn from four schools in the same district as the previous experiments. The pool of stimulus words and sentences was the same as in Experiment 7 but there were some modifications to the procedure. For each subject, training and control words were assigned at random from the pool without being pretested as in Experiment 7. There were two training trials, both conducted in the same session, and on the following day the

Table 6 Effect on word retention of variation in sentence context: Experiment 8

	Context	
	Low	High
Training: Mean percentage reading accuracy on training words		
Trial 1	76	91
Trial 2	94	99
Retention: Difference in mean percentage accuracy between training and control words (Control percentage accuracy in parentheses)		
Word reading	23 (58)	22 (63)
Spelling completion First vowel	20 (39)	8 (44)
Second vowel	5 (32)	5 (34)

retention test was conducted. This was identical in form to that in the previous experiment. Eight subjects were randomly assigned to each of the six experimental conditions.

The results are shown in Table 6. Accuracy was greater in the high than the low context condition in both the first and second training trials (0.001 level of significance). In the retention word reading test there was not a significant difference between the high and low context in the extent to which training word accuracy exceeded controls in word reading. This was the same for the three word reading test conditions. However, in spelling completion of the first vowel letter the training-control retention *difference* was smaller under the high than the low context condition (significant at the 0.02 level). In spelling completion of the second vowel letter neither training-control difference was significantly greater than zero.

For these 8-year-old readers in Experiment 8 the evidence shows a compensatory relationship between the contributions of context and knowledge of orthographic components. Knowledge of the first vowel letter of words was poorer under high than low levels of context. The availability of context reduced the quality of correctly generated associations, lowering retention of knowledge of particular orthographic components which were required for *spelling*. This finding is consistent with the results reported by Ehri & Roberts (1979). The evidence, however, from Experiments 7 and 8 reported above fails to support the proposition that there is a similar compensatory relationship between the current contributions of context and of the other classes of knowledge for generation procedures in *reading*.

Recall

The generation procedures, which have been considered in some detail, enable a reading response to be given to a print word where no stored orthographic representation of the print word is available. The recall procedures, which will now be considered in detail, enable a reading response to be made from a stored representation of the print word. This is a representation of the sequence of letters which comprise the print word, that is the acquired orthographic representation of the word. The recall procedures also normally involve relations between this orthographic representation and meaning(s) of the word, that is the semantic representation of the word. First, consideration will be given to the recall procedures for accessing the acquired orthographic representation of a word. Subsequently, consideration will be given to those aspects of the procedures by which connections are formed between the accessed orthographic representation and the semantic representation of the word.

Access of orthographic representations of words: Priority of boundary letters

In this theoretical account, the recall procedures to access the orthographic representation of a word are not only different from generation procedures but are based on different parsing of the stimulus information and unit formation. Recall procedures are based on letters as units and are largely independent of sublexical phonological units such as phonemes.

For accessing the stored orthographic representation of a word, the letters in the left and right boundary positions of the word take priority over internal letters. This priority is also largely independent of any parsing of letters based on sublexical phonology. It is, for example, independent of whether the initial letters relate to a single phoneme, e.g. sh-, or two phonemes, e.g. st-. Some of the information stored from the reader's experience of print words is used to form sublexical relations between orthographic components and sublexical phonological components for generation procedures. Most of these relations are not, however, used for recall procedures involved in accessing the orthographic representation of a word. See Figure 1. Recall procedures are based on specific stored representations which are rapidly accessed and unlike generation procedures do not involve pooling of information from various representations as in the formation of sublexical relations. Recall procedures are carried out largely independently of submorphemic phonological components of words. The significant components in recall procedures for access to the orthographic representation of the word are letters and their positions in relation to the two boundaries of the print word. The recall procedures give priority to these boundary letters and to letter length of the word.

Some evidence about these theoretical assertions was obtained in Experiment 9 in which children were presented with pseudohomophones for oral reading under speed instructions. Pseudohomophones, e.g. 'maik', can elicit the same oral reading response as homophonically related words, e.g. 'make', when generation procedures are used that take into account information on relationships between letters and phonological components of the word. Alternatively, recall procedures, as described here, could be used to respond to such pseudohomophone items. If so, responses would not be restricted to those that are homophonic but may include any words, with the same left and right boundary letters and of closely similar letter length, for which the reader has acquired an orthographic representation.

The subjects of Experiment 9 were 87 children aged 7 years 0 months to 7 years 11 months with reading ages of 7 years 0 months to 8 years 11 months (New Zealand standardisation of the Burt Word Reading Test). They were drawn from seven schools which used the approach to teaching of reading previously described. A set of 20 monosyllabic pseudohomophones, e.g. 'maik', was presented for rapid oral reading. The speed instructions were designed to reduce the opportunity for using generation procedures which are expected to require more time than the faster recall procedures. In addition, 20 items, e.g. 'make', which were the homophonically matched words, were also presented for rapid reading prior to presentation of the set of pseudohomophones. This procedure provided a check on whether any failure to give accurate homophonic responses (e.g. *make*) to the pseudohomophone stimuli (e.g. 'maik') could be attributed to lack of experience of the pronunciation or meaning of the homophonically matched word (e.g. 'make').

Table 7 The percentage of subjects making homophonic and non-homophonic responses in rapid reading of pseudohomophones: Experiment 9

Stimulus	Accurate homophonic response	Most common non-homophonic substitution errors		Accuracy for homophonically matched word	
maik	15	milk	74	make	97
lite	30	little, late, lit	51	light	91
nise	37	noise, nurse, nose	46	nice	97
trane	43	turn	25	train	86
whight	44	weight	21	white	92
nite	48	nit, neat	21	night	100
lait	59	light, lit, let	18	late	89
bote	64	bottle	13	boat	100

Notes: (1) The accurate homophonic response is the homophonically matched word. (2) Where there is more than one common non-homophonic error, the percentage given is the total for those shown. (3) The response in all cases is the initial response to the item.

Results are reported for those pseudohomophones for which the homophonically matched word was read correctly by more than 85% of subjects. Fourteen of the 20 pseudohomophone items fulfilled this criterion. (The six excluded were: fense, quight, seet, sope, wate, woak.) Among the 14 items there were eight which received accurate homophonic responses from fewer than 70% of subjects. These items are listed in Table 7, along with the most common non-homophonic substitution errors. The remaining six items, along with the percentage of subjects making accurate homophonic responses, were: cleen 95, nead 82, sleap 78, mouce 78, roap 77, horce 76. It may be noted that with the exception of 'roap' these items differed from the homophonically matched word by only one letter in one medial (non-boundary) position within the word. In contrast, among the items listed in Table 7, which were those yielding fewer accurate homophonic responses, only one ('nise') had such close letter similarity with the homophonically matched word. It is apparent that it was largely only those pseudohomophone items with a close letter similarity to the homophonically matched word which received a high incidence of apparent homophonic responses. These responses could in fact be due to recall procedures, which as described in the present theory, are based on letter information, with priority given to boundary letters, and largely independent of relationships between letters and phonological components of the word.

The principal interest, however, is in the responses to the stimulus items listed in Table 7. These responses were consistent with the account of the present theory in which recall procedures are based on letters as units, and letters in boundary positions receive priority, as well as letter length of the word. The boundary letters of the responses, but not internal letters, matched the stimuli, and the letter length was close to that of the stimuli. Moreover, the fact that these frequently occurring substitutions were not homophonic with the stimulus words indicates that procedures have been used which make little use of relations between letters and (submorphemic) phonological components of words. While the substitutions were consistent with this account, some of them do indicate use of one particular kind of relation between letters and phonological components of words. This involved the 'silent e' (vowel marker) letter on the right boundary. See the following items: 'trane' (response *turn*), 'nite' (responses *nit*, *neat*). On the evidence of these substitution errors it appears that while recall procedures give priority to left and right boundary letters and word length, the procedures are not entirely independent of relationships between the boundary letters and corresponding phonological components of the word. The letter 'e' in the right boundary is apparently recognised as sometimes having no corresponding phoneme in this position. Hence for items such as 'trane', 'nite', responses were produced which did not have orthographic forms with a final letter 'e'. Whether or not recall procedures are independent of other particular relationships between boundary letters and phonological components is considered in Experiments 10 to 12 in the next section.

An alternative interpretation to the present data is that such could be explained not by priority given to boundary letters in recall procedures but simply by the children not having acquired any orthographic representation of the internal letters for the stimulus word and the words which are given as substitution responses. There are no data in Experiment 9 to test this interpretation for 7-year-old readers. However, this alternative interpretation is not plausible when applied to results of the experiments of Jordan (1990) and McCusker et al. (1981). In these experiments moderately high frequency words were presented to adult readers. The results indicated that boundary letters received processing priority.

Access of orthographic representations of words independent of phonology

The purpose of this series of experiments was to examine whether or not in recall procedures the letters of a word are processed without reference to their relationships with phonological components of the word. For example, consider the letter 's' as both the left boundary letter of a word and also the initial member of the consonant digraph spelling unit 'sh' which corresponds to a single phoneme, /ʃ/. In contrast, consider the letter 's' as a member of the initial letter cluster 'st' where such corresponds to two phonemes /s/ and /t/. If the relationships between letters and phoneme components of words are always significant in recall procedures, then any visual or temporal interference within a digraph spelling unit, e.g. 'sh' would be expected to be more disruptive to reading recall performance than the same interference between successive letters, each of which represents a phoneme. Pring (1981) investigated the existence of digraph processing units but her experiments were relevant only to generation procedures, not recall.

In Experiment 10, stimulus words were presented to 40 8-year-olds and 40 adults for rapid oral reading. The stimuli were monosyllabic words with initial consonant digraphs (e.g. short, child, thing, while) and words with initial letters which were not digraphs (e.g. stay, clown, dress, great). Half the subjects formed one experimental group which saw all these words intact, and the rest of the subjects saw them with a visual interferer, e.g. 'c%hild'. Within each group half the subjects were presented with the words in lower case and half in upper case. Reaction times were measured from shutter opening, which exposed the image of the word projected from a slide, to microphone detection of onset of a vocal reading response. The shutter closed at onset of vocalisation.

The main results were the same for both age groups and for both lower case and upper case. There were slower reading response times as a result of the interference and a greater response time increase for words with initial 'th' digraphs (e.g. 'thing') than either words with other initial digraphs (e.g. 'short') or words without (e.g. 'stay'). The effect of the interferer did not differ between words with other initial digraphs (sh, ch, and wh) and words without initial digraphs. Hence the only differential effect was specific to words with the initial 'th' digraph. This digraph is of exceedingly high frequency in the initial position of English words. Also, the 'th' words used in the experiment were themselves of higher frequency than most of the other stimulus words.

Experiment 11 was designed to determine the reaction time to words with an initial 'th' compared to words without an initial' 'th' digraph, when the sets of words are matched on word frequency. It was also designed to examine whether the differentially greater visual interference effect for initial 'th' words was specific to the particular interferer used. Hence in Experiment 11 one third of the subjects were presented with intact words, a third with words containing a new visual interferer, e.g. 't≭hing'. The remaining third of the subjects received the stimuli with the same visual interferer used in Experiment 10. All words were presented in lower case. In total, there were 51 8-year-olds and 51 adults. Although the visual interferer used in the previous experiment showed a similar differential effect, specific to the 'th' digraph, the new interferer showed no such reliable differential effect, even though the new interferer had as much effect as the old on reaction time to non-digraph words. Hence it was concluded that the effect with initial 'th'. which in Experiment 10 was the only obtained differential effect between words with and without initial digraphs, was specific to the particular visual interferer, '%'. This has a salient, nearly vertical, line feature which probably greatly interfered with the visual analysis of the preceding 't' and/or following 'h' which also both have a salient vertical line feature. This differentially greater effect is of course independent of any relationship between letters and the phoneme or cluster of phonemes to which they correspond.

These two experiments using visual interferers gave no grounds to reject the theoretical account that recall procedures to access the orthographic representation of a word are based on letters as units and are largely independent of relationships between initial position letters and the phonemes to which they may correspond. Experiment 12 in this series was designed to further examine the question using temporal rather than visual interference. This temporal interference was introduced between the first two letters of words with, and words without, initial consonant digraphs.

In the first part of Experiment 12 thirty-two adult subjects were given tachistoscopic (unmasked) presentations of monosyllabic words, including 20 with initial digraphs 'sh', 'ch', 'th' and 20 matched words with initial non-digraph clusters, 'st', 'cl', 'tr'. The number of stimulus items which formed a word when the initial letter was removed were equated between the two sets of items. Half the subjects saw the words presented intact and the other half saw the words with a 100 millisecond delay between presentation of the initial letter and the rest of the word (presented without the initial letter). Each of the two parts were presented in the normal spatial location for equal exposure times. Exposure times for both groups of subjects were adjusted over preliminary trials for each subject to give an approximate 50% whole word accuracy rate for free written report. The average exposure times so determined were 11 milliseconds for the intact condition and 15 milliseconds for each of the two parts of the word in the delay condition.

The results shown in Table 8 give the accuracy for reports of both initial two letters, irrespective of the accuracy of the report of the rest of the word. There were no statistically significant differences between accuracy for digraphs (e.g. sh) and nondigraphs (e.g. st) The evidence was consistent with the theoretical account offered here. In recall procedures the left boundary letter of a word is processed independently of its relationship with phoneme units.

The second part of Experiment 12 was conducted to test the prediction

Table 8 Mean percentage accuracy for both initial two
letters of items in tachistoscopic identification:
Experiment 12

Stimulus condition	Digraphs	Nondigraphs
Words		
Intact	78	77
Delay	57	61
Pseudowords		
Intact	88	79
Delay	63	68

from the present theoretical account that the relationship between the letters and
phonological components of the word would have an influence in generation
procedures. As pseudowords do not have a representation which can be recalled,
generation procedures are required for accurate responses to such items. A further group of 32 adult subjects were given tachistoscopic presentations of 20
pseudowords with initial consonant digraphs and 20 with nondigraphs. The initial two letters of each item were the same as for the word items in the first part
of this experiment. The items were formed by interchanging the initial letter
pairs between these word items. For example, 'shick' was formed from the word
'chick' and a word with initial 'sh'. The subjects were informed that the stimulus items were pseudowords. All other aspects of the presentation conditions and
procedure were the same as in the first part of this experiment. The average
exposure times for the intact and delay conditions were also the same as in the
first part of the experiment.

The results, given in Table 8, show an advantage for digraphs over nondigraphs when these are intact in the tachistoscopic presentation but no such
advantage in the delay condition. (Statistically significant interaction at the 0.02
level.) An analysis of errors to the second letter of items with initial nondigraphs showed that this advantage was not due to a general bias to respond
with the letter 'h' for the second letter position of the pseudowords. Such a bias
was a possibility when a large proportion of the stimuli, namely those with initial digraphs, had 'h' in this position. It was concluded that the advantage for initial digraphs (e.g. sh) relative to nondigraphs (e.g. st) in pseudowords was a
consequence of the initial two letters being processed as a unit by virtue of each
digraph being related to a single phoneme. This influence of the relationships
between letters and phonological components is predicted by the present theory

but only in generation procedures. Such procedures are required in responding to pseudowords. Such processing units based on relationships between initial position letters and phonemes are not predicted for recall procedures, as used in responding to known print words. No evidence for these was found in Experiments 10–12. It was concluded that units larger than a single letter (but smaller than the print morpheme) can be used in generation procedures, while letters are the normal units of recall procedures. These findings contradict the theoretical account of Ehri (1992) in which recall of a print word is made from word-specific 'visual–phonologic' representations involving connections between letters and phonemes. These findings on recall procedures are about access to the stored orthographic representation of words. Those aspects of the recall procedures by which the accessed orthographic representation makes connection with the meaning(s) of the word will be considered next.

Access of word meaning via the phonological lexicon

In a theoretical account of any cognitive skill one of the important issues is how the acquired skill is linked with existing knowledge and skills. When the child is acquiring orthographic representations of words, the meanings of most of these words will be available to the child in previously stored knowledge. An important question is how these word meanings are accessed by the new skill of reading. What links are formed between the newly acquired and stored orthographic representation of words and existing stored representations of word meanings? In recall procedures there are two principal possibilities. The first is that a direct connection is formed between the new orthographic representation of the print word and the existing representations of the meaning(s) of the word, bypassing any direct connection with the existing representation in the child's phonological lexicon. The second possibility is that access to word meaning is made via the representation in the existing phonological lexicon which is activated by the stored orthographic representation of the word. The representation in the phonological lexicon is specific to a whole word or morpheme, and is the point of access of the new skill of print word identification to the existing knowledge of meanings of words. Some evidence will be presented (Experiments 13–15) which shows that the second possibility operates some, if not all, of the time as a recall procedure in reading (although it is possible that at times both procedures may operate in parallel).

Consideration of recall procedures suffers from confusions in many conceptual analyses (e.g. Van Orden *et al.*, 1988) as they take dual route theories as their point of reference. In this class of theories there are two processing alternatives: (i) word meanings accessed directly from the acquired orthographic representation of the word, and (ii) word meanings accessed via the representation of the word in the child's phonological lexicon, when this representation is activated through sublexical phonological mediation. Such a conceptual analysis confuses generation procedures and recall procedures. For generation procedures, access to the word meaning(s) is necessarily via a representation in the phonological lexicon. An orthographic representation of the word does not exist. It is yet to be acquired and phonological mediation of one form or another is the principal procedure. The issue here, however, is about recall procedures, not generation procedures. In recall procedures there is not only the possibility of accessing the word meaning directly from the stored orthographic representation of the print word but, as already suggested, the possibility that access of word meaning is via the representation in the phonological lexicon activated by the stored orthographic representation. This alternative has been considered explicitly by Patterson & Coltheart (1987).

Given this second alternative, there is the additional possibility of a 'spelling check' procedure. See Figure 3. Having accessed word meanings via the representation in the phonological lexicon, it may be possible to use connections between the representations of the word meanings and the associated orthographic representations, for the purpose of checking which meaning applies. This would be useful for distinguishing meanings of (non-homographic) homophones, e.g. 'scene', 'seen'. These connections could be acquired through experience of spelling the words.

The purpose of Experiment 13 was to obtain some evidence which would discriminate between the theoretical alternatives. The experimental reading task involved semantic decisions. The subject judged whether a correct or incorrect meaning was given for a word, e.g. 'scene — used eyes'. In this item, although 'scene' is homophonic with 'seen', the subject is required to consider the orthographic information and reject the item as incorrect. Other correct items were also presented, e.g. 'grow — get bigger'. If the reader were able to use a recall procedure and this was exclusively direct access to word meanings from stored orthographic representations of the words, then responses to the homophonic items would be expected to be as accurate as to non-homophonic control items. On the other hand, if in recall procedures, readers exclusively access meanings of words via representations in the phonological lexicon, then they would fail to exceed chance performance on the homophonic items. But if, in addition, a 'spelling check' (see Figure 3) were available, accuracy would vary according to the relative thresholds for activation of the alternative meanings of the phonological word and the resulting spelling checks. Achievement of accuracy on this semantic decision task will be enhanced by any spelling check which indicates a mismatch between the orthographic representation of the stimulus word, e.g. SCENE, and an orthographic representation, e.g. SEEN,

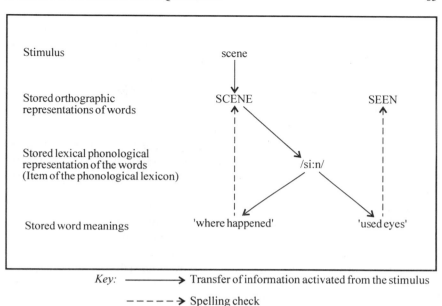

Stimulus   scene

Stored orthographic   SCENE   SEEN
representations of words

Stored lexical phonological
representation of the words   /siːn/
(Item of the phonological lexicon)

Stored word meanings   'where happened'   'used eyes'

Key: ———→ Transfer of information activated from the stimulus

– – – – → Spelling check

Figure 3 Example of access of word meanings via the phonological lexicon postulated for recall procedures of word identification in reading.

activated by one of the alternative meanings of the phonological word, e.g. 'used eyes'. If readers were exclusively using generation rather than recall procedures, no spelling check would be possible as stored orthographic representations of words are only involved in recall procedures, not in generation procedures. If using only generation, then the reader's performance on the homophonic items of the semantic decision task would not be above chance level.

In this decision task the spelling checks would be more effective the lower the threshold for activation of a mismatched orthographic representation, e.g. SEEN, relative to the threshold for a matched orthographic representation, e.g. SCENE, activated by the other word meaning, e.g. 'where happened'. High word frequency would give some indication of low threshold. Hence it would be expected that if such spelling checks function in reading recall procedures, then semantic decisions in this task would be more accurate the greater the positive difference between: (a) the word frequency of the corresponding homophone (not presented), e.g. 'seen', which is homophonic with the stimulus word, e.g. 'scene', and (b) the frequency of the stimulus word.

On the other hand, under the alternative theoretical account of recall as exclusively direct access to word meaning from the stored orthographic representation, no such relationship would be expected involving the corresponding homophones. It would be expected that because of the greater opportunity to acquire direct access connections, high frequency stimulus words would result in higher decision accuracy than low frequency words.

The subjects for Experiment 13 were 79 children with reading comprehension attainments within the average range. They were drawn from the schools which used the same 'book experience' approach to teaching reading which was previously described. Thirty-one of the children were aged 8 years and 48 aged 11 years. They responded to a set of 60 semantic decision items, 15 of which were incorrect experimental items, e.g. 'scene — used eyes', 15 control items, also incorrect, and 30 correct filler items, e.g. 'grow — get bigger'. To reduce the opportunities for exclusive use of generation procedures, all experimental and control target words contained at least one irregular letter–sound correspondence. Item order was randomised. The subjects judged for each item whether the meaning given, e.g. 'used eyes', was correct for the target word, e.g. 'scene'. Word frequencies for the target words in the experimental items and their corresponding homophone (not presented) were obtained from the Carroll *et al.* (1971) lists for grade 3 texts. To provide a measure amenable to linear correlation statistics, a logarithmic transformation, $\log_{10} (f + 10)$, of the raw frequencies, f, was made. For each item a frequency difference was calculated by subtracting the transformed frequency measure for the stimulus word, e.g. 'scene' from that for the corresponding appropriate homophone, e.g. 'seen' (not presented). This frequency measure difference was correlated with the average percentage correct decision responses for each experimental item of the semantic decision task. The correlation was statistically significant, $r = +0.54$ ($p < 0.05$). The correlation between the frequency measure for the stimulus words and the percentage correct responses for each was negative but not statistically significant, $r = -0.43$. These results are consistent with the theoretical alternative which proposes that at times access to word meaning is via the phonological lexicon, with spelling checks being initiated from the activated word meanings. The results are inconsistent with the exclusive use of direct access to word meaning from the stored orthographic representation.

The responses to the experimental items were compared with matched control words. These were controls for 'graphemic similarity' between the experimental target word (e.g. 'scene') and the appropriate word (e.g. 'seen'). The target words of the control items were matched with those of the experimental items on 'graphemic similarity' (Weber, 1970) in the following way. The target words in the control items (e.g. 'sewn' in 'sewn — used eyes') had an average

Table 9 Mean percentage accuracy of semantic decisions: Experiment 13

	8 years	11 years
Matched controls	82	95
Experimental homophones	66	81

degree of 'graphemic similarity' with the appropriate words (e.g. 'seen') which was matched to the degree of similarity between the experimental targets (e.g. 'scene' in 'scene — used eyes') and the appropriate words (e.g. 'seen').

The accuracy levels on experimental and control items of the semantic decision task are given in Table 9. The accuracy level was above chance for both age levels. It was lower for the experimental homophone items than the matched controls ($p < 0.001$ in both analyses by subjects and by items). This difference was not significantly greater for the 8-year-olds than the 11-years-olds ($p > 0.30$ in both analyses). The results are contrary to that expected if the readers were exclusively using generation procedures.

Although graphemic similarity has been controlled in Experiment 13, there remains the possibility that between the experimental homophone and matched control items there was a difference in either meaningfulness or word recognition difficulty for the subjects. To examine whether this had been the case, a control experiment was conducted, Experiment 14. Each target word from the experimental and control items of Experiment 13 was presented with four alternative meanings, e.g. 'scene — (a) looked at, (b) cooked well, (c) pile of stones, (d) view of place'. Subjects selected the alternative which they judged to be the best meaning for the target word. The subjects were drawn from the same schools as the subjects in Experiment 13 and were of the same age and reading comprehension attainment level. For the 8-year-olds the mean percentage accuracy for selecting meanings for the words of the experimental items was 75% and for the words of the control items, 76% (difference not statistically significant); for the 11-year-olds the level of accuracy was 90% for both sets of words. Hence neither level of meaningfulness nor word recognition difficulty appear to differ between the experimental and control items Such factors are not an explanation of the results of Experiment 13.

In the next experiment of the series, Experiment 15, the generality of the results of Experiment 13 was examined using a task requiring a semantic decision about a sentence instead of about a target word and given meaning. Subjects judged whether each sentence made sense in its presented orthographic form. There were 15 semantically incorrect experimental sentences, e.g. 'She had not scene the book before'; 15 semantically incorrect sentences which were controls for graphemic similarity, e.g. 'She had not sewn the book before'; and 30 semantically correct filler sentences, e.g. 'She wanted to cut the flowers'. The subjects were the same as in Experiment 13. The differences in response accuracy between the experimental and control sentences in this decision task were as great (in the same direction) as those obtained in the semantic decision task of Experiment 13. The correlations between the frequency measure for the target words of the experimental sentences and decision response accuracy were also very similar. The word frequency measure for the target word, e.g. 'scene', was subtracted from that for the corresponding homophone, e.g. 'seen' (not presented). This difference in frequency measure was correlated with the average percentage correct decision responses for each experimental sentence. The correlation was statistically significant, $r = +0.53$ ($p < 0.05$). The correlation between the frequency measure for the target word and the percentage correct decision responses for each sentence was negative, $r = -0.40$, but not statistically significant.

The results with this task using semantic decisions about sentences show that the findings with the semantic decision task of Experiment 13 can be generalised to full sentence contexts. Both sets of results are inconsistent with the theoretical proposition that recall procedures in reading involve exclusively direct access from the stored orthographic representation of the print word to word meaning. The results are, however, consistent with the theoretical proposition that access from the stored orthographic representation of the word to existing meanings of the word will at times occur via the existing phonological lexicon. Where necessary, as in distinguishing homophones, subsequent spelling checks are initiated from the activated word meanings.

Summary

A theoretical account was given of acquisition of the skill of word identification in reading an alphabetic orthography. The emphasis was on reading as a cognitive skill. Two classes of procedures for word identification responses were postulated: recall and generation. The outcomes of generation, along with teacher provided associations, are the sources of knowledge for recall. Unlike dual route theory, this account has an explicit concern with sources of knowledge used in generation and in recall procedures.

A series of experiments was conducted to test predictions from the theory regarding the learner's sources of knowledge for generation. They were conducted with average five- and six-year-old children who received school reading instruction without explicit phonics. Evidence was obtained that from their limited stored print word experience they induced sublexical relations between orthographic and phonological components specific to position within the word, and that these relations were a source of knowledge for generation procedures. Moreover, these sublexical relations were used by the learners for generation procedures when they did not use independent letter–phoneme correspondences, which do not depend on lexical experiences but are provided by phonics instruction. Results were obtained which could not be explained by any of the theories of Goswami & Bryant, Ehri, or Seidenberg & McClelland.

Experiments were also conducted to examine what knowledge might transfer from existing or concurrent skills. Neither letter names nor sound-to-letter knowledge from spelling were found to be sources of specific letter–phoneme correspondence knowledge for generation procedures in reading. They may have, however, general facilitative effects on phonemic segmentation and identity at an earlier level of learning. In generation procedures the relationships between the contributions of knowledge from different sources was examined. While evidence for a compensatory relationship between the sources for generation was not obtained for reading, the availability of context sometimes reduced the quality of correctly generated associations as manifest in spelling performance.

Another series of experiments was conducted to test the theoretical account of the nature of recall procedures in print word identification. These procedures access stored orthographic representations of words and the evidence indicated that this access was carried out via letter units and largely independently of phonological components of words. Some evidence was presented to show that in recall procedures, access from stored orthographic representations of words to existing meanings of words does not always occur directly but at times via the reader's existing phonological lexicon and a subsequent 'spelling check' procedure.

Acknowledgments

The second author held a New Zealand University Grants Committee Postdoctoral Fellowship for work in collaboration with the first author. During this time Dr Fletcher-Flinn collaborated in the genesis of the theoretical work on sublexical relations and prepared and conducted Experiment 2. She prepared and conducted preliminary pilots for Experiments 4, 5 and 6, and contributed to the conduct of Experiments 13 to 15.

David Cottrell, now at the University of Western Sydney, also held a New Zealand University Grants Committee Postdoctoral Fellowship for work in collaboration with the first author. Dr Cottrell prepared and conducted Experiments 1, and 3 to 6 during this collaboration.

Rhona Johnston, Department of Psychology, University of St Andrews, provided the initiative which in turn led to Experiments 13 to 15.

Steve Cassidy, Department of Computer Science, Victoria University of Wellington, provided the data analyses for the grapheme frequency counts from reading books. These counts were used in Experiments 1 to 4.

Both authors received Victoria University of Wellington Internal Research Grants which assisted in the conduct of this work. A grant from the British Council assisted in the travel and ensuing contact which enabled the planning of Experiments 13 to 15.

The authors thank the school authorities, staff and children for their willing cooperation throughout these studies.

References

Backman, J., Bruck, M., Hebert, M. and Seidenberg, M. S. (1984) Acquisition and use of spelling-sound correspondences in reading. *Journal of Experimental Child Psychology* 38, 114–33.

Baron, J. (1977) Mechanisms for pronouncing printed words: Use and acquisition. In D. LaBerge and S. J. Samuels (eds) *Basic Processes in Reading: Perception and Comprehension* (pp. 175–216). Hillsdale, NJ: Erlbaum.

Bradley, L. and Bryant, P. E. (1979) Independence of reading and spelling in backward and normal readers. *Developmental Medicine and Child Neurology* 21, 504–14.

Bryant, P. E. and Bradley, L. (1980) Why children sometimes write words which they do not read. In U. Frith (ed.) *Cognitive Processes in Spelling* (pp. 355–70). London: Academic Press.

Byrne, B. and Fielding-Barnsley, R. (1989) Phonemic awareness and letter knowledge in the child's acquisition of the alphabetic principle. *Journal of Educational Psychology* 81, 313–21.

— (1990) Acquiring the alphabetic principle: A case for teaching recognition of phoneme identity. *Journal of Educational Psychology* 82, 805–12.

Carroll, J. B., Davies, P. and Richman, B. (1971) *The American Heritage Word Frequency Book*. Boston: Houghton Mifflin.

Cassidy, S. (1990) *Early Reading Development: A Computational View* (Tech. Rep. No. CS-TR-90-8 (SC)). Wellington, New Zealand: Victoria University of Wellington, Department of Computer Science.

Coltheart, M. (1978) Lexical access in simple reading tasks. In G. Underwood (ed.) *Strategies of Information Processing* (pp. 151–216). London: Academic Press.
— (1980) Reading, phonological recoding and deep dyslexia. In M. Coltheart, K. Patterson and J. C. Marshall (eds) *Deep Dyslexia* (pp. 197–226). London: Routledge & Kegan Paul.
Department of Education (1985) *Reading in Junior Classes*. Wellington, New Zealand: Departmnt of Education.
Ehri, L. C. (1987) Learning to read and spell words. *Journal of Reading Behavior* 19, 5–31.
— (1992) Reconceptualizing the development of sight word reading and its relationship to recoding. In P. B. Gough, L. C. Ehri and R. Treiman (eds) *Reading Acquisition* (pp. 107–43). Hillsdale, NJ: Erlbaum.
Ehri, L. C. and Roberts, K. T. (1979) Do beginners learn printed words better in contexts or in isolation? *Child Development* 50, 675–85.
Ehri, L. C. and Wilce, L. S. (1985) Movement into reading: Is the first stage of printed word learning visual or phonetic? *Reading Research Quarterly* 20, 163–79.
Fletcher-Flinn, C. M., Thompson, G. B. and Cottrell, D. S. (1992) Learning letter-sound correspondences: The acquisition of sublexical relations in reading disabled and young normal readers. Manuscript submitted for publication.
Frith, U. (1985) Beneath the surface of developmental dyslexia. In K. E. Patterson, J. C. Marshall and M. Coltheart (eds) *Surface Dyslexia: Neuropsychological and Cognitive Studies of Phonological Reading* (pp. 301–30). London: Erlbaum.
Glushko, R. J. (1979) The organization and activation of orthographic knowledge in reading aloud. *Journal of Experimental Psychology: Human Perception and Performance* 5, 674–91.
Goswami, U. and Bryant, P. (1990) *Phonological Skills and Learning to Read*. Hove, UK: Erlbaum.
Holligan, C. and Johnston, R. S. (1988) The use of phonological information by good and poor readers in memory and reading tasks. *Memory & Cognition* 16, 522–32.
Johnston, R. S., Thompson, G. B., Fletcher-Flinn, C. M. and Holligan, C. (1992) The function of phonology in the acquisition of reading: Lexical and sentence processing. Manuscript submitted for publication.
Jordan, T. J. (1990) Presenting words without interior letters: Superiority over single letters and influence of postmask boundaries. *Journal of Experimental Psychology: Human Perception and Performance* 16, 893–909.
Jorm, A. F. and Share, D. L. (1983). Phonological recoding and reading acquisition. *Applied Psycholinguistics* 4, 103–47.
Marsh, G., Friedman, M., Welch, V. and Desberg, P. (1981) A cognitive–developmental theory of reading acquisition. In G. E. MacKinnon and T. G. Waller (eds) *Reading Research: Advances in Theory and Practice* Vol. 3. (pp. 199–221). New York: Academic Press.
Mason, J. M. (1984) Early reading from a developmental perspective. In P. D. Pearson (ed.) *Handbook of Reading Research* (pp. 505–43). New York: Longman.
McCusker, L. X., Gough, P. B. and Bias, R. G. (1981) Word recognition inside out and outside in. *Journal of Experimental Psychology: Human Perception and Performance* 7, 538–51.
McCusker, L. X., Hillinger, M. L. and Bias, R. G. (1981) Phonological recoding and reading. *Psychological Bulletin* 89, 217–45.
Mitchell, D. C. (1982) *The Process of Reading: A Cognitive Analysis of Fluent Reading and Learning to Read*. Chichester, UK: Wiley.
Patterson, K. and Coltheart, V. (1987) Phonological processes in reading: a tutorial

review. In M. Coltheart (ed.) *The Psychology of Reading. Attention and Performance XII* (pp. 421–47). Hillsdale, NJ: Erlbaum.

Perfetti, C. A. (1985) *Reading Ability.* New York: Oxford University Press.

Perfetti, C. A. and Bell, L. (1991) Phonemic activation during the first 40 ms of word identification: Evidence from backward masking and priming. *Journal of Memory and Language* 30, 473–85.

Perfetti, C. A., Bell, L. and Delaney, S. (1988) Automatic phonetic activation in silent word reading: Evidence from backward masking. *Journal of Memory and Language* 27, 59–70.

Pick, A. D., Unze, M. G., Brownell, C. A., Drozdel, J. G. and Hopmann, M. R. (1978) Young children's knowledge of word structure. *Child Development* 49, 669–80.

Pring, L. (1981) Phonological codes and functional spelling units: reality and implications. *Perception & Psychophysics* 30, 573–8.

Rayner, K. and Pollatsek, A. (1989) *The Psychology of Reading.* Englewood Cliffs, NJ: Prentice Hall.

Read, C. (1986) *Children's Creative Spelling.* London: Routledge & Kegan Paul.

Scott, J. A. and Ehri, L. C. (1990) Sight word reading in prereaders: Use of logographic vs. alphabetic access routes. *Journal of Reading Behavior* 22, 149–66.

Seidenberg, M. S. (1985) The time course of information activation and utilization in visual word recognition. In D. Besner, T. G. Waller and G. E. MacKinnon (eds) *Reading Research: Advances in Theory and Practice* Vol. 5. (pp. 199–252). New York: Academic Press.

Seidenberg, M. S. and McClelland, J. L. (1989) A distributed, developmental model of word recognition and naming. *Psychological Review* 96, 523–68.

Seymour, P. H. K. (1990) Developmental dyslexia. In M. W. Eysenck (ed.) *Cognitive Psychology: An International Review.* Chichester, UK: Wiley.

Seymour, P. H. K. and Elder, L. (1986) Beginning reading without phonology. *Cognitive Neuropsychology* 3, 1–36.

Seymour, P. H. K. and MacGregor, J. C. (1984) Developmental dyslexia: A cognitive experimental analysis of phonological, morphemic, and visual impairments. *Cognitive Neuropsychology* 1, 43–82.

Stanovich, K. E. (1986) Matthew effects in reading: Some consequences of individual differences in the acquisition of literacy. *Reading Research Quarterly* 11, 360–406.

Stuart, M. and Coltheart, M. (1988) Does reading develop in a sequence of stages? *Cognition* 30, 139–81.

Thompson, G. B., Cottrell D. S. and Fletcher-Flinn, C. M. (1991) Sublexical relations in the acquisition of reading skill . Unpublished manuscript.

Thompson, G. B., Fletcher-Flinn, C. M. and Cottrell, D. S. (1991) Sources of grapheme–phoneme correspondence knowledge during the acquisition of reading and spelling. Unpublished manuscript.

Van Orden, G. C., Johnston, J. C. and Hale, B. L. (1988) Word identification in reading proceeds from spelling to sound to meaning. *Journal of Experimental Psychology: Learning, Memory and Cognition* 14, 371–86.

Van Orden, G. C., Pennington, B. F. and Stone, G. O. (1990) Word identification in reading and the promise of subsymbolic psycholinguistics. *Psychological Review* 97, 488–522.

Venezky, R. L. (1975) The curious role of letter names in reading instruction. *Visible Language* 9, 7–23.

Vernon, P. E. (1977) *Graded Word Spelling Test.* London: Hodder & Stoughton.

Waters, G. S., Seidenberg, M. S. and Bruck, M. (1984) Children's and adults' use of spelling-sound information in three reading tasks. *Memory & Cognition* 12, 293–305.
Weber, R. (1970) A linguistic analysis of first-grade reading errors. *Reading Research Quarterly* 5, 427–51.

3 The Effects of Type of Instruction on Processes of Reading Acquisition

G. BRIAN THOMPSON AND RHONA S. JOHNSTON

Importance of the Issue

A traditional concern in research on reading acquisition has been the effect of different types of instruction on the rate of progress in learning. A more recent concern is the influence of the type of instruction on the way the child attempts to learn. This issue may be considered independently of rate of learning, in so far as children of the same level of reading attainment may vary in the extent of their use of different processes or attempted ways of learning. For example, one child may be attempting to identify many printed words by recoding the letters into the code of their corresponding speech sounds, which are then used to make a reading response. Another child, of the same level of reading acquisition, may attempt the same words in a different way. This child may not recode letters into codes of speech sounds but may recall a stored association between the learned representation of the sequence of letters and an existing representation of the sound or meaning of the word.

When alternative processes or ways of responding such as these are a possibility, a question arises about the extent to which different types of instruction influence children to use each kind of process. There are two important reasons for attempting to answer this question. The first derives from attempts to compare the effectiveness of different kinds of reading instruction; the second from attempts to test theories of reading acquisition.

Comparison of the effectiveness of types of reading instruction

Where the effectiveness of different types of instruction is expected to derive from the learners' use of different processes, evidence of this effectiveness cannot be given merely by demonstrating better attainment; evidence is also required that the processes, or ways of learning, are in fact different under the different kinds of instruction. For example, the set of 27 US Office of Education Cooperative Reading Studies (Bond & Dykstra, 1967) included comparisons of reading instruction which emphasised phonics with instruction that did not. While it would be expected that the children's processes of learning would be different under these different types of instruction, the studies did not provide evidence of this, only evidence about the reading attainment levels under the different kinds of instruction. While doubt was expressed about what conclusions could be drawn from these studies (Dykstra, 1968; Corder, 1971), and also earlier studies reviewed by Chall (1967), claims continue to be made that instruction which includes systematic teaching of phonics produces higher attainment levels of word identification in reading than instruction which does not (Chall, 1979; Guthrie & Tyler, 1978; Adams, 1990). Interpretation of these claims remains ambiguous without evidence about differences in the children's processes of learning under the different types of instruction.

The differences in attainment levels could arise from factors other than differences in the children's processing. For example, the schools which choose to emphasise phonics instruction may have had a higher probability of being schools which have a more than average concern to raise reading standards and have provided more steeply graduated levels of reading instruction which demand faster overall progress in the attainment of the students. Any claimed better reading attainment may derive from a number of associated factors, such as this difference in levels of difficulty of instruction provided (or time and resources devoted to the instruction) rather than any specific difference in the children's processes of learning.

Testing theories of reading acquisition

There is a second reason for the importance of considering the influence of type of instruction on processes of learning. It derives from the requirements for testing theories of reading acquisition. Several current theories about acquisition of reading attempt to give accounts of the processes used by readers and how the processes are claimed to differ at successive levels or phases of skill acquisition, from the initial to the mature (Frith, 1985; Seymour & MacGregor, 1984; Seymour, 1990). If teaching methods have some influence on the processes used by readers, then tests of these theories would need to take account of the teaching methods to which children are exposed. Tests of the theories obtained from studies conducted on children exposed to one teaching method may support a particular theory but those obtained from children exposed to a

Table 1 Hypothetical examples of children's use of a particular learning process under different types of instruction

Levels of reading skill	Prediction from theory	Type of Instruction	
		A	B
Level 1	Not used	Not used	Used
Level 2	Used	Used	Used

different teaching method may be inconsistent with the theory. See the hypothetical example in Table 1. At the first level of reading skill a research result that tests the theory is consistent with the theory when the research is conducted with children receiving Type A instruction but inconsistent when conducted with children receiving Type B instruction.

There are two matters which are particularly troublesome. The first problem is that the theory itself may, unwittingly, reflect the methods of teaching reading with which the theorist is familiar. Furthermore, the theory may reflect the teaching method experienced by the children who are the subjects of the empirical studies used to test the theory. In other words, theory construction and testing may be a self-reflective, and self-deluding exercise. Moreover, the theory may derive from the same beliefs which have influenced the educators who provide the method of teaching experienced by the children on whom the theory is tested. There are hazards of circularity inherent in this method of theory construction and testing. One way to reduce the hazards would be to also test the theory on children exposed to reading methods derived from a different set of beliefs.

Second, current theories are notable in the absence of specification of how the child's use of the reading processes would vary under different teaching methods. This matter is one that needs to be addressed before any progress can be made on the first problem. The theory of reading acquisition presented by Thompson and Fletcher-Flinn in Chapter 2 of this volume is taken here as a framework for attempting such a specification.

A Theoretical Specification of the Effects of Phonics Instruction

While the above arguments can be applied to any type of reading instruction, much of the traditional research interest has been in the comparison of reading instruction which includes an emphasis on phonics with instruction that largely excludes explicit phonics tuition. There has, however, been much interest recently in the effects on subsequent reading attainments of instruction in phonological segmentation skills (Goswami & Bryant, 1990). This chapter will be confined to the traditional research interest of the effects of phonics instruction. Phonics instruction is here defined as explicit teaching about individual letter–sound correspondences, their sequences (including spelling patterns), and the pronunciation of corresponding sounds.

There are recent influential theoretical accounts of reading acquisition (Frith, 1985; Gough & Hillinger, 1980) which provide a justification for phonics teaching, implying that such phonics instruction will enhance the effectiveness of learning to read. However, neither account should be interpreted as suggesting that learning of reading will not proceed without explicit phonics instruction. Frith is specific on this point, stating that children may acquire letter–sound correspondences through their experiences of attempting to spell words without receiving phonics instruction. (The evidence, however, presented in Chapter 2 shows that this is not the case.) These theoretical accounts have not included any explicit specification of how learning processes of children may differ qualitatively between those children exposed to phonics instruction and those not.

The theory of knowledge sources and procedures for reading acquisition in Chapter 2 of this volume is used here as a basis for specifying in what ways processing would be expected to differ for children receiving explicit phonics instruction. In this theory there are two classes of procedures for word identification in reading, recall procedures and generation procedures. Recall is from representations of the letters of the word which are stored as a consequence of experience with the particular print word. Generation procedures can result in a response when recall procedures have been insufficient. In the theory there are three classes of sources of knowledge for generation procedures:

(a) 'Sublexical relations' between orthographic (letter code) and phonological (sound code) components, induced from stored experience of print words and their phonological components.
(b) 'Provided letter–sound correspondences' where these are available, as in phonics instruction.
(c) Semantic and syntactic context of the stimulus word.

See Chapter 2 of this volume.

The propositions put forward here about the effects of explicit phonics instruction, and the limits of those effects, are:

(i) The direct effects of phonics instruction are restricted to influences on the use of generation procedures and do not extend directly to recall procedures of word identification in reading.

(ii)   The exposure to phonics instruction tends to increase the learner's attempts
       at obtaining a reading response from generation procedures, beyond that
       which is obtainable by the learner from recall procedures alone. The gener-
       ation procedures of children receiving phonics instruction will have 'pro-
       vided letter-sound correspondences' among the sources of knowledge.
(iii) Although less frequently attempting to obtain a response from generation
       procedures, learners receiving instruction without explicit phonics will still
       be able to make sufficient use of generation procedures when necessary in
       reading connected text. These generation procedures will have 'sublexical
       relations', but not 'provided letter–sound correspondences' among the
       sources of knowledge.

In the remainder of this chapter evidence about these propositions is examined.

The Evidence

It is plausible that the extent and nature of use of generation procedures
could change as the level of reading skill acquisition increases. See Table 1.
Hence the learner's level of reading attainment needs to be controlled when
examining the influence of types of instruction on processes relevant to word
identification in reading. Unfortunately, such control has been rare in published
work. Most of the published studies which have examined the influence of
phonics instruction on processes of reading do so by considering response failures. They classify the learner's errors of oral reading. The distribution of various classes of errors for students exposed to phonics instruction is compared
with that of students not receiving such instruction (Barr, 1975; DeLawter,
1975; Dank, 1977; Elder, 1971). Among these studies only that by Elder provides data which enable comparisons of the instructional methods for students
at matched levels of reading attainment. His data were collected in 1962–64
from a sample of 7-year-old students in Scotland (West Lothian), who were
exposed to beginning reading instruction with a strong phonics component, and
a sample matched by reading attainment level from schools in Michigan, USA,
where there was no such emphasis on phonics. While the overall word identification accuracy on oral reading passages was not significantly different, the
children receiving the phonics instruction had a significantly higher percentage
of nonword responses among their errors. Moreover, they had a significantly
lower percentage of real word substitutions than the children not receiving the
phonics emphasis. This result is consistent with the proposition that phonics
instruction tends to increase the learner's attempts at generation. Nonword
error responses would be the product of attempts to obtain a response from
generation procedures where recall has not been sufficient. At least some of the

real word substitutions could be the result of the reader not attempting to obtain a reading response from generation procedures when recall has failed. The substitution errors made would be the product of this recall failure. This interpretation is also consistent with the finding by Elder that the children receiving phonics instruction read paragraphs orally at a significantly slower rate (mean rate 87 words per minute) than the children not exposed to a phonics emphasis (mean rate 101 words per minute). This difference could be attributed to the additional time taken in attempting to obtain a response from generation procedures by the children receiving phonics.

A study by Lesgold *et al.* (1985), provides further data on speed of responding. In this study reaction times were measured for the oral reading of each one of a set of words. Only reaction time data for correct responses were included. In the data, which were collected in 1977-79, comparisons were available between children provided with instruction having a phonics emphasis (including synthetic phonics, i.e. 'blending') and children exposed to a 'basal reader' programme without a phonics emphasis. Both groups were in the United States and from similar social environments. As the data were reported in subgroups by reading attainment level, it was possible to compare children who received the different methods of reading instruction but were at approximately the same reading accuracy level on the experimental oral word reading task. At Grade 1 level those receiving the instruction with a phonics emphasis showed much slower reaction times (for correct responses) than those subjects not receiving this emphasis (Accuracy level at 60–70%). At subsequent Grade levels, when the accuracy levels were matched there was no difference in reaction times between the children receiving the different methods.

Hence explicit phonics instruction had a discernable influence on the procedures used for correct reading responses by children in their initial year of reading instruction. The slower reaction time by those learners receiving phonics instruction is consistent with the interpretation that a larger proportion of their correct responses were the outcome of generation procedures from which these learners more frequently attempted to obtain a response than those not receiving phonics instruction. The time to execute a reading response obtained from generation procedures, is greater than that for responses obtained from recall procedures (See Chapter 2 in this volume). In the first year of reading instruction an appreciable proportion of *correct* responses are likely to be obtained from generation procedures. Hence reading reaction times will be slow. If learners exposed to phonics instruction obtain a larger proportion of their correct responses from generation procedures, then their reaction times will be slower than for learners not receiving such phonics. In subsequent years of instruction, whether including phonics or not, only a small proportion of *correct* responses are likely to be obtained from generation procedures. All average progress learners will then

have received enough experience of print words to obtain most of their correct
responses from recall procedures.

It has been claimed (Elder, 1971) that children exposed to instruction with
a phonics emphasis make less use of semantic and syntactic context of a word as
a source of information for reading responses. However, the data presented were
restricted to classifications of students' errors of oral reading. Potter (1980) has
shown that scores of syntactic acceptability of oral reading errors can be the
same when the errors are made to words presented in a list as they are when the
words belong to connected text. From the fact that a reader makes a syntactically
or semantically acceptable error it cannot be concluded that the reader has used
syntactic or semantic information in their processing which leads to the
response. Evidence of a more satisfactory kind is required. In Chapter 2 a
method was described for examining the contribution of context to generation
procedures (Experiments 7 and 8 in that chapter). This method could also be
employed to compare the contributions of contextual information to generation
procedures of learners receiving phonics instruction and learners who do not.
Until such comparisons are made no conclusion can be drawn about the claim
that children receiving phonics instruction make more limited use of syntactic
and semantic context as a source of information for reading responses.

New evidence on generation procedures

If phonics instruction tends to increase the learner's attempts at obtaining a
response from generation procedures, then such learners would be expected to
be at a disadvantage when required to respond to a task which required only
attempted reading recall, and generation procedures were inappropriate. There is
such a reading task, a 'lexical decision' task, in which the subject decides
whether or not each item is a real (orthographically correct) word. Half the items
are such words, a quarter of them are ordinary nonwords, e.g. 'blum', and a
quarter are pseudohomophones, e.g. 'blud', which sound like words but are
orthographically incorrect. If the reader's decision in this task were obtained
from generation procedures, then the pseudohomophone would be classified
(erroneously) as a correct word. Hence if phonics instruction increases the learner's attempts at obtaining a reading response from generation procedures there
would be a lower incidence of correct reading decisions on pseudohomophones
in this task among learners exposed to phonics instruction than among those not.
An experiment of Johnston & Thompson (1989) showed such a difference. Two
groups were compared: 40 8-year-old children in Fife, Scotland, who had
received systematic phonics tuition as part of their school reading instruction
and 70 children of the same age in a suburban area of New Zealand who had

received the 'book experience' approach to reading instruction (New Zealand Department of Education, 1985) which did not include explicit phonics instruction. The essentials of this approach had been in use in New Zealand schools for at least 25 years (see Appendix). Both groups of children were English-speaking and were matched on levels of word reading attainment.

The items for this task were selected to take account of vowel pronunciation differences between the countries. There were 40 real words, 20 ordinary nonwords and 20 pseudohomophones. The latter two sets of items were selected to fulfil Taft's (1982) criteria for matching pairs of items by visual similarity to real words. Also, the two sets of items were derived from words with the same mean frequencies (Carroll *et al.*, 1971, Grade 3 norms). Each item was presented on an individual card in a random order for each subject. The subjects sorted the words into those that were considered 'real words' and those that were 'made-up words'. Demonstration items were presented in which the experimenter showed that some of the items (the pseudohomophones) sounded the same as real words but were spelt incorrectly and should be classified as a 'made-up word'.

The results are shown in Table 2, Experiment 1. There was a lower incidence of correct reading decisions for pseudohomophones than ordinary nonwords by the children receiving phonics instruction. However, there was not a significant difference between the two classes of items for the New Zealand children who did not receive school phonics instruction. (The interaction between the two instructional groups and classes of items was statistically significant at the 0.01 level for both analyses by subjects and by items.)

Results are also available for further samples from the same school populations (Johnston, Thompson, Fletcher-Flinn & Holligan, 1992). In this, Experiment 2, there were two groups of 30 $8^{1}/_{2}$-year-old subjects matched on level of attainment in reading comprehension. The stimulus items were the same as in Experiment 1 but were presented as a list for silent reading by the subjects, who were instructed to place a tick beside those they classified as 'real words' and a cross beside the 'made-up' words. The pattern of results was the same as in Experiment 1. See Table 2. The results of both experiments are consistent with the proposition about the effects of phonics instruction on processes of reading. Learners receiving phonics instruction tend to have a higher incidence of attempts at obtaining a reading response from generation procedures, beyond what is obtainable from recall procedures. In spite of these differences, however, a large proportion of responses by both instructional groups in Experiment 1 and 2 are apparently obtained by recall procedures rather than generation procedures. If responses had been obtained exclusively by generation procedures then the accuracy level for decisions on pseudohomophones would be in the range 0% to 50%. This was not the case. The accuracy for the children receiving phonics

Table 2 Lexical decision and sentence decision: Mean percentage of items correct for 8-year-olds (Standard deviations in brackets)

Class of items	Lexical decision				Sentence decision	
	Experiment 1		Experiment 2		Experiment 4	
	Phonics	No phonics	Phonics	No phonics	Phonics	No phonics
Ordinary nonwords	82 (14)	82 (14)	91 (11)	91 (7)	84 (16)	88 (14)
Pseudohomophones	69 (19)	78 (17)	80 (15)	88 (12)	76 (19)	79 (17)
	—	—	—	—	—	—
Percentage point difference	13	4	11	3	8	9

instruction was in the range 70% to 80% and higher again for those not receiving phonics.

For the children not receiving phonics instruction the results could be given an alternative interpretation. It may be argued that these children, because they have not received phonics instruction, are much slower than those who have, in acquiring knowledge of the relationships between letters and phonological components of words which is used in generation procedures. By this argument the New Zealand children at eight years of age, through this claimed lack of knowledge, may not show the influence of generation procedures in this task but older New Zealand children with more reading experience may gain this knowledge by inducing it themselves. These children would then be expected to show the influence of generation procedures. Results were obtained in Experiment 2 for 11-year-olds, as well as 8-year-olds, which enables a test of this alternative interpretation. Two instructional groups of 35 11-year-olds were matched on level of attainment in reading comprehension. Contrary to the expectation of this alternative interpretation, level of accuracy of decisions on pseudohomophone items was as high (95%) for the New Zealand subjects not receiving phonics as it was for the Scottish subjects receiving phonics (94%). (Difference between the instructional groups was not statistically significant.)

While erroneous decisions about the pseudohomophone (e.g. 'blud') in this task are more likely with increased attempts at responding from generation procedures, accuracy of decisions about the ordinary nonwords (e.g. 'blum') would not be affected. Generation procedures, adequately used, cannot result in *word* identification for items which are true nonwords. Hence generation procedures which are attempted more often by children receiving phonics instruction would give them no disadvantage (or advantage) for these items in lexical decisions. Recall procedures, if adequately used, will always fail to produce a reading identification response to nonwords. In this reading decision task recognition of this failure is all that is needed to make a (correct) decision that the item is not a word. The results of both Experiments 1 and 2 are consistent with this argument. The level of accuracy of decisions on ordinary nonwords by the 8-year-olds was the same for the Scottish group receiving phonics as for the New Zealand children who did not. See Table 2. (It was also not significantly different for the 11-year-olds in Experiment 2.)

In summary, several features of the results of Experiments 1 and 2 are consistent with the proposition that explicit phonics instruction tends to increase the learner's attempts at obtaining a reading response from generation procedures, beyond what is obtainable by the learner from recall procedures alone. However, this proposition does not logically imply that children not receiving phonics are unable to make sufficient use of generation procedures in reading when required. Indeed, in the theory employed here it is explicit that learners have two other sources of knowledge for generation procedures which do not depend on phonics instruction. The evidence for one of these sources, sublexical relations, is considered in Chapter 2 of this volume. This evidence was from experimental studies conducted with children in New Zealand schools who had not received phonics instruction. It was consistent with the third proposition about the effects of phonics instruction examined in this chapter. This proposition implies that learners receiving instruction without explicit phonics tuition will be capable of using generation procedures when necessary.

The influence of phonics instruction on the learner's capability at using generation procedures for obtaining a response to single words was examined in Experiment 3 (Johnston & Thompson, 1989). In the experimental task, attempts at obtaining a response by generation procedures were obligatory as recall procedures were not sufficient. The subjects were presented with the ordinary nonwords (e.g. 'blum') and the pseudohomophones (e.g. 'blud') of Experiment 1, and decided whether or not each item 'sounds the same as a real word'. Unlike the lexical decision task of Experiments 1 and 2, recall procedures alone would not be sufficient for high accuracy. The task was administered to the two groups of 8-year-olds subjects who participated in Experiment 1. The group which did not receive phonics showed some discrimination between the pseudohomophones and ordinary nonwords in this task. It is most unlikely that this discrimination could have been achieved with responses obtained from recall procedures alone. The ordinary nonword and the pseudohomophone items were matched on both visual similarity and word frequency. However, this group without phonics instruction was not as accurate as the group who received phonics. The group without phonics was able to make some use of generation procedures but not as effectively as the children receiving phonics instruction. Moreover, when subsequently required to read aloud the items that they had classified as sounding like words, the children without phonics performed much worse than those children receiving phonics. Nevertheless, both these tasks and the lexical decision task in Experiments 1 and 2 require responses to single words. Results with tasks involving only single words may not generalise to the reading of text, where words are embedded in the semantic and syntactic context of sentences.

Experiment 4 was designed to examine this question. Each pseudohomophone and nonword item of Experiments 1 and 2 was embedded in a sentence, e.g. 'There is blud on the floor' (for the pseudohomophone 'blud'); 'The flowers are in blum early' (for the ordinary nonword 'blum'). These sentences were presented in random sequences along with an equal number of correct sentences, e.g. 'The cat lay on the bed.' The subject's task was to read each sentence and decided whether or not it made sense. Demonstration items were presented in which the experimenter showed that some of the sentences (those with a pseudohomophone) *sounded* all right but contained a word, e.g. 'blud', which was spelt incorrectly. It was pointed out that such items should be classified as 'not making sense'. The subjects were the 8-year-olds who participated in Experiment 2.

The results of Experiment 4, however, were different from those of the lexical decision task in Experiment 2. See Table 2. The children who did not receive school phonics instruction, as well as those who did, showed a lower incidence of correct decisions for sentences with pseudohomophones than sentences with ordinary nonwords. (This main effect was statistically significant at the 0.001 level for the analysis by subjects and 0.025 level for the analysis by items. There was no significant interaction between this effect and the instructional groups. Nor was there a significant main effect of instructional groups).

There are two plausible strategies for carrying out this task. In the first, the reader attempts to identify all items of the sentence, including the ordinary nonword or the pseudohomophone, to determine the possible meaning for the sentence. In this strategy, attempts are made at obtaining word identification responses by generation procedures if recall procedures are not sufficient. If this strategy were used it would be expected that the incidence of correct performance on sentences with a pseudohomophone would be lower than for sentences with an ordinary nonword. In the second strategy the subject scans each sentence to determine whether it contains any items to which the subject is unable to make a response by recall procedures. Any sentence containing such an item is then rejected as not making sense to the reader. In this strategy no attempts are made at obtaining responses by generation procedures. If this strategy were used exclusively, the incidence of correct performance on sentences with a pseudohomophone would be expected to be not significantly different from that on sentences with ordinary nonwords. The results were consistent with the first strategy for both the 8-year-old children receiving phonics as well as for those without phonics.

This result on the items embedded in sentences, for the children without phonics instruction, is in contrast to their performance in Experiments 1 and 2 in which decisions were made about the items as single words without a sentence context. In that task, for which generation procedures were not obligatory, unlike the children who received phonics instruction, those without phonics apparently did not attempt reading responses from generation procedures, recall procedures being used almost exclusively. However, for those children, when the items were embedded in sentence contexts and a task strategy used which involves attempts at obtaining responses by generation procedures, performance relating to pseudohomophones was lower than that relating to ordinary nonwords. Semantic and syntactic context can be a source of knowledge contributing to generation procedures. It is likely that such contextual influences in generation procedures have occurred for these children in this sentence decision task. Any such contextual influence on the difference in performance between items involving pseudowords and those involving ordinary nonwords would be likely to be an influence on generation rather than recall procedures. The pseudowords and ordinary nonwords were matched on both visual similarity to real words and word frequency of such. If there were any contextual influence on recall procedures, this item matching would tend to equate that influence between the two classes of items.

So, the results of Experiment 4 demonstrate that in a task in which sentence context is available and a 'reading for meaning' strategy adopted, 8-year-olds who have not received phonics instruction are capable of using generation procedures and show this capability in the task to the same extent as children of matched reading comprehension attainment level who have received phonics instruction. This finding is consistent with the third proposition about the effects of phonics instruction. Although less frequently attempting to obtain a response from generation procedures, learners receiving instruction without phonics will still be able to make sufficient use of generation procedures when necessary in reading connected text.

Recall procedures

It now remains to consider the first proposition about the effects of phonics instruction. This stated that the effects are restricted to influences on the use of generation procedures and do not extend directly to recall procedures of word identification in reading. The second part of this proposition cannot be considered without some specification of the nature of recall procedures. Two main possibilities were considered in Chapter 2 by Thompson & Fletcher-Flinn. The first is that a direct connection is formed between the acquired representation of the letters of the print word and the reader's existing representation of the meaning of the word, bypassing any direct connection with the existing representation in the child's phonological lexicon. The second possibility is that in recall procedures access to word meaning is made via the existing phonological lexicon and a subsequent spelling check procedure. (This lexical phonological representation is specific to a whole word and access to the representation is an internal process not implying pronunciation of the word nor access to component sounds.) In Chapter 2 evidence was reported which was consistent with the child at times using the latter procedures but not direct connections exclusively. The evidence reported there was from children who had not received school phonics instruction. The expectation from the above proposition would be that children who received phonics instruction would show the same results. Evidence is also available for children receiving phonics instruction (Johnston, Thompson, Fletcher-Flinn & Holligan, 1992). The 8- and 11-year-old subjects were the same as in Experiment 2 above. The experimental reading task involved decisions about the meaningfulness of sentences containing a target homophone, e.g. 'She had not scene the book before'. Refer to Experiment 15 in Chapter 2 by Thompson & Fletcher-Flinn for the detailed rationale which will not be repeated here. It is sufficient to state that the results were the same for the group of children exposed to phonics as for those not receiving explicit phonics. The correlation between the average percentage correct decision responses for each experimental item and the difference between frequencies of the homophone of the target and the target was + 0.47 for the phonics group and + 0.58 for the group without phonics. These positive correlations are consistent with the child's use of the phonological lexicon and a subsequent spelling check procedure. The correlation between the percentage correct decision responses for each item and the frequency for the target word was −0.46 and −0.42 respectively. Positive rather than the obtained negative correlations were expected if direct connections were used exclusively in recall procedures. (The differences between these pairs of correlations were not statistically significant.)

In addition, mean accuracy of decisions about the meaningfulness of sentences containing homophones was compared with sentences containing control items matched to the homophones on both visual similarity and word frequency. There was significantly lower accuracy on the homophone items than the controls in both instructional groups ($p < 0.001$ in the analysis by subjects and $p < 0.01$ in the analysis by items). The differences relative to controls did not vary significantly between the instructional groups at either 8 or 11 years of age. Moreover, this difference did not vary significantly between the 8- and 11-year-olds in either instructional group. A control experiment (Experiment 14 in Chapter 2) was also conducted to obtain a measure of any remaining differences between the experimental homophones and matched controls in either meaningfulness or word recognition difficulty for the two groups of subjects. With this measure as a covariate a further analysis was made of these results on reading decision accuracy. The pattern of results remained the same. There was no variation in the homophone versus control differences between instructional groups at either 8 or 11 years of ages. The results are consistent with the proposal that in recall procedures access to existing meanings of words sometimes occurs via the reader's existing phonological lexicon.

The evidence previously considered and the results of these comparisons between the instructional groups are consistent with the proposition that the effects of phonics instruction are restricted to influences on the generation procedures of word identification and do not extend directly to the recall procedures.

Summary

The question considered was whether or not the processes or ways of learning are different under different types of reading instruction. In particular, an examination was made of the effects of phonics, as a component of reading instruction, on the processes of reading acquisition. The theory of knowledge sources and procedures for reading acquisition in Chapter 2 by Thompson & Fletcher-Flinn was used as a basis for deriving a theoretical specification about the effects of explicit phonics instruction and the limits of those effects. There were three propositions: (i) The effects of phonics instruction are restricted to influences on the use of generation procedures of word identification and do not extend directly to recall procedures; (ii) the exposure to phonics instruction tends to increase the learner's attempts at obtaining a reading response from generation procedures, beyond that which is obtainable by the reader from recall procedures alone; (iii) although less frequently attempting to obtain a response from generation procedures, learners receiving instruction without explicit phonics will still be able to make sufficient use of generation procedures when necessary in reading connected text. Evidence was presented which was consistent with these propositions about the effects of explicit phonics instruction and the limits of those effects.

Acknowledgements

The authors are indebted to Christopher Holligan, Craigie College of Education, Scotland, and Claire Fletcher-Flinn, University of Auckland, New Zealand, who contributed to the conduct of several of these experiments.

The first author received Victoria University of Wellington Internal Research Grants which assisted in the conduct of this work. Grants from the British Council to both authors assisted in the travel and ensuing contact which enabled the planning and conduct of the experiments.

The authors thank the school authorities, staff and children for their willing cooperation throughout these studies.

References

Adams, M. J. (1990) *Beginning to Read: Thinking and Learning about Print*. Cambridge, MA: MIT Press.

Barr, R. (1975) The effect of instruction on pupil reading strategies. *Reading Research Quarterly* 10, 555–82.

Bond, G. L. and Dykstra, R. (1967) The cooperative research program in first-grade reading instruction. *Reading Research Quarterly* 2, (4), 5–142.

Carroll, J. B., Davies, P. and Richman, B. (1971) *The American Heritage Word Frequency Book*. Boston: Houghton Mifflin.

Chall, J. S. (1967) *Learning to Read: The Great Debate*. New York: McGraw Hill.

— (1979) The great debate: Ten years later, with a modest proposal for reading stages. In L. B. Resnick and P. A. Weaver (eds) *Theory and Practice of Early Reading* Vol. 1 (pp. 29–55). Hillsdale, NJ: Erlbaum.

Corder, R. (1971) The information base for reading. HEW Office of Education Final Report, Project No. 0-9031. Berkeley, CA: Educational Testing Service. (ERIC Document Reproduction Service No. ED 054922.)

Dank, M. (1977) What effect do reading programs have on the oral reading behavior of children? *Reading Improvement* 14, 66–9.

DeLawter, J. A. (1975) The relationship of beginning reading instruction and miscue patterns. In W. D. Page (ed.) *Help for the Reading Teacher: New Directions in Research* (pp. 42–51). Urbana, Ill: ERIC Clearinghouse on Reading and Communication Skills/National Conference on Research in English.

Dykstra, R. (1968) The effectiveness of code- and meaning-emphasis beginning reading programs. *Reading Teacher* 22, 17–23.

Elder, R. D. (1971) Oral reading achievement of Scottish and American children. *Elementary School Journal* 71, 216–30.

Frith, U. (1985) Beneath the surface of developmental dyslexia. In K. E. Patterson, J. C. Marshall and M. Coltheart (eds) *Surface Dyslexia: Neuropsychological and Cognitive Studies of Phonological Reading* (pp. 301–30). London: Erlbaum.

Goswami, U. and Bryant, P. (1990) *Phonological Skills and Learning to Read*. Hove, UK: Erlbaum.

Gough, P. B. and Hillinger, M. L. (1980) Learning to read: An unnatural act. *Bulletin of The Orton Society* 30, 179–96.

Guthrie, J. T. and Tyler, S. J. (1978) Cognition and instruction for poor readers. *Journal of Reading Behavior* 10, 57–78.

Johnston, R. S. and Thompson, G. B. (1989) Is dependence on phonological information in children's reading a product of instructional approach? *Journal of Experimental Child Psychology* 48, 131–45.

Johnston, R. S., Thompson, G. B., Fletcher-Flinn, C. M. and Holligan, C. (1992) The function of phonology in the acquisition of reading: Lexical and sentence processing. Manuscript submitted for publication.

Lesgold, A., Resnick, L. B. and Hammond, K. (1985) Learning to read: A longitudinal study of word skill development in two curricula. In G. E. MacKinnon and T. G. Waller (eds) *Reading Research: Advances in Theory and Practice* Vol. 4 (pp. 107–38). New York: Academic Press.

New Zealand Department of Education (1985) *Reading in Junior Classes*. Wellington, New Zealand: Department of Education.

Potter, F. (1980) Miscue analysis: A cautionary note. *Journal of Research in Reading* 3, 116–28.

Seymour, P. H. K. (1990) Developmental dyslexia. In M. W. Eysenck (ed.) *Cognitive Psychology: An International Review*. Chichester, UK: Wiley.

Seymour, P. H. K. and MacGregor, J. C. (1984) Developmental dyslexia: A cognitive experimental analysis of phonological, morphemic, and visual impairments. *Cognitive Neuropsychology* 1, 43–82.

Taft, M. (1982) An alternative to grapheme-phoneme conversion rules? *Memory & Cognition* 10, 465–74.

4   The Case Against Context

TOM NICHOLSON

Introduction

The purpose of this chapter is to review evidence which suggests that the use of context clues by beginning readers is not the real reason for success in learning to read and, in the case of some children, may actually be a sign of reading difficulty.

Such an opening statement seems to fly in the face of reality, given that beginning readers often use context as a strategy to help recognise words. Yet the surprising finding from research on this issue is that context is a strategy used more by poor readers than good. This is due to the fact that poor readers are poor decoders, and therefore have no choice but to rely on context in order to compensate for their poor decoding skills (Stanovich, 1980). If this is the case, and it seems to be, then it is hard to accept that the use of context is a major factor in learning to read.

However, popular opinion is more in line with everyday experience, which suggests that the use of context clues is what makes readers good. According to Stanovich (1986), there are three kinds of arguments that support the popular view. First, it is argued that good readers are good at using context for general comprehension. So it is inferred that they must use it for recognising words as well. Second, it is argued that good readers are able to use context clues to avoid having to read all the print on the page. Third, it is argued that being good at using context must be the reason why good readers are good.

Yet, as Stanovich (1986) also points out, the error in this reasoning is to think that ability to use context is therefore the key reason for the good reader's success. Correlation is assumed to mean causation. And this is where research and popular opinion drift apart. If popular opinion were correct, then research should also show that poor readers are less able to use context to help recognise words. But this is not so. Stanovich (1986) cites numerous studies which show that poor readers use context, sometimes even more than good readers. Now if poor readers are also good at using context, then why are they not good readers?

To understand this discrepancy more clearly, the rest of this chapter will focus on the influence of a specific study, carried out by Ken Goodman in 1965, which looked at the role of linguistic cues in reading. The results of this study, soon to be discussed, showed that children were able to read words in context more easily than in isolation. It is a classic study, cited widely in support of popular thinking on how children read. So, given that it runs against the grain of research cited by Stanovich (1986), it is an important study to revisit.

A Classic Study

There is little doubt that the Goodman study has become a 'classic'. It has been cited at least 85 times (Staff, 1986), and it has also been reprinted in the new edition of *Theoretical Models and Processes of Reading* (Singer & Ruddell, 1985). The study was also mentioned in the latter publication, by Samuels (1985), who stated that, 'Goodman's (1965) study of word recognition of words in isolation and in context must be classified as one of the most influential studies ever published on beginning reading' (p. 265).

A similar comment on the influence of the study was also made by Pearson (1978), that 'It is rare to pick up an article dealing with the influence of context on word recognition without finding a reference to Goodman's (1965) article, "A Linguistic Study of Cues and Miscues in Reading". It has become a classic' (pp. 355–6).

Blanchard (1979), in a critique of the Goodman (1965) study, also mentioned that 'It is doubtful that Goodman intended or envisioned "classic" status for his research. Nevertheless, the implications have gained a wide and captive audience among educational theorists and practitioners' (p. 71). But is the Goodman (1965) study still being cited by theorists and practitioners? The answer is yes. An example can be found in a recent language textbook by Lindfors (1987):

There is increasing evidence that children draw heavily on this knowledge of language structure when they read also. In one well-known reading study of one hundred first-, second-, and third-grade children, the researcher first determined each child's reading level and then gave each child words to read orally at that level (Goodman, 1965: 74).

The subjects for Goodman's (1965) study were 100 children, from Grades 1–3, in an inner city school in Detroit. The procedure was to read lists of words taken from their basal readers, until they reached a list of appropriate difficulty. Then the children read the basal reader from which the words were taken. The results

Table 1 Average word errors in list and in story (based on Goodman, 1965)

Grade	List Average	Story Average	% gain*
1	9.5	3.4	64
2	20.1	5.1	75
3	18.8	3.4	82

* Gain can be calculated by using the following procedure:

$$\frac{\text{difference in average scores}}{\text{list average score}} \times 100$$

For example, in Grade 1:

$$\frac{9.5 - 3.4}{9.5} \times 100 = 64.2\%$$

were based on a comparison of the average number of mistakes on the same words, from the list and from the story.

What Goodman found was that Grade 1 children gained about 64% when reading words in story context compared with an isolated list. In Grade 2, the gain was about 75%, and in Grade 3, the improvement was about 82% (see Table 1). For example, at Grade 1 level, Goodman found that children made an average of 9.5 errors on list, but only 3.4 errors in context. As a percentage, this meant that only about a third as many errors were made in context as in list, or, as Goodman (1965) put it, 'Average first graders could read almost two out of three words in the story which they missed on the list' (p. 641).

Sparks of Disagreement

Yet a number of researchers have challenged these results. Pearson (1978) questioned the size of the improvement in context, given that he and his graduate students, after two replication studies, had been unable to obtain the same dramatic gains:

> In two replications, our best estimates are 40 per cent for first grade students and 55–60 per cent for third grade students. Furthermore we have found that we can get a 20 per cent improvement just by letting students read the list twice ... Correcting for the improvement from sheer exposure

to the list a second time, it would seem reasonable to assign a 20 to 30 per cent benefit to context (not 60 to 80 per cent) (p. 356).

Allington (1978) also obtained results that did not fit with Goodman's findings. Allington asked fourth graders to read a passage where the words were in random order, and also the same passage where the words were in normal order. In this study, half of the children read the jumbled passage first, and half read the normal passage first. The results showed that, in terms of errors, poor readers gained from context, but good readers did not. These results suggested that Goodman's findings may have been partly due to the order in which children completed the reading tasks, that is, words in list, followed by words in context. The results also suggested that poor readers relied more on context clues than did good readers.

Negin (1981) looked at the effect of order of testing on use of context. In this study, children either read list before context (list–story), context before list (story–list), or list before list (list–list). The findings were that average readers in Grades 1 and 3 made least gains in the list–list testing, and made most gains in the list–story testing. Interestingly, however, the children made slightly negative gains in the story–list testing. The study also showed that list–story gains were much reduced when children read difficult stories, whereas list–list gains actually increased. With story–list, there were still slightly negative gains, even for the difficult stories. Later in this chapter we will discuss further research which suggests that children's ability to read words better in context depends on whether they read list before context, or vice versa.

However, in addition to the above replication studies, Stanovich (1986) has reviewed many experimental, or 'lab'-type studies, which have shown that context helps poor readers just as much as good readers. For example, Stanovich, Cunningham & Feeman (1984), in a longitudinal study of first-graders, found that, 'less skilled readers were getting as much contextual facilitation as were the skilled readers, when the latter were at a similar level of context free decoding ability' (p. 668). Put more simply, the study found that good readers made more gains in context, as against a list, at the start of first grade. But at that stage, they were also better at reading lists than were the poor readers. Later in the year, however, when the poor readers were able to match the earlier scores of the good readers in list reading, the poor readers were also able to achieve the same gains in context. So poor readers were able to use context just as well as good readers when they were matched in their ability to read word lists, that is, in their ability to decode words out of context.

In another cross-sectional study, involving children from Grades 3 to 5, Adams & Huggins (1985) looked at the ability to use context to guess irregularly spelled words, for example 'ocean' in the sentence 'the ship sailed across the *ocean*'. They found that children were better able to read such words in context, no matter what their age or reading level. But they also concluded that 'when adjusted for the ability to recognise words in isolation, use of context did not appear to vary with overall reading proficiency' (p. 262). In other words, like the Stanovich *et al.* (1984) study, it was initially found that good readers made bigger gains in context than did poor readers, but that they were not evenly matched in their ability to read the lists. However, when Adams & Huggins looked at the relationship between reading ability and context gains they found negative correlations, that is children made less use of context as reading ability improved. In short, these findings seem to be consistent with the argument so far, that beginning and poorer readers are just as likely to use context, when the task is of similar difficulty level. In addition, the use of context is actually likely to decrease as reading ability improves.

In a recent review of this debate, I have also concluded that use of context is more likely in less skilled readers (Nicholson, 1986). However, in his defence, Goodman (1987) has disagreed with the kind of evidence presented so far, arguing that these different results have relied on 'contrived contexts' instead of 'real texts':

> Now here's a puzzle. How is it possible that Philip Gough, P. David Pearson and Tom Nicholson, among a host of other respected researchers could have found in their research that children are more successful reading isolated words? The answer, *in every case*, is that they did not use real texts in their studies. These are researchers who believe they must control the variables in their studies. So they contrived *contexts*. In the study by Singer, Samuels and Spiroff which was the first to challenge my findings, the contexts were three word sentences: e.g. The bat flies. In Nicholson's case, he creates a kind of cloze, leaves holes in his abbreviated and specially constructed texts, and believes he has a more controlled context in which to test out my `psycholinguistic guessing game' theory (p. 6).

Replications Using 'Real Texts'

So the debate continues. In the remainder of this chapter, we will look at some further replication studies that have taken Goodman's criticisms seriously. The first study, by Nicholson, Lillas & Rzoska (1988), was intended to replicate the classic study as closely as possible, and to avoid 'contrived contexts'. The reading material came from an informal prose test (Department of Education, 1985), consisting of a series of short texts ranging from 76 to 189 words in length, taken from stories published for use in schools. The word lists were constructed by typing the words in these stories in backwards order. That is, each

Table 2 Average word errors in list and in story context (based on Nicholson
et al., 1988)

Age	*n*	Reading level	List average	Context average	% gain*
6	8	poor	7.3	3.5	52
	8	good	7.5	4.3	43
8	8	poor	10.5	5.0	52
	8	good	5.9	6.3	−7

* Gain was calculated as shown in Table 1.

list started with the last word and finished with the first word. For example
'There was once a little house...' would become 'house little a once was there'.

There were thirty-two children in the study, including six-year-olds and
eight-year-olds, in four equal groups according to age and reading level. So
there were eight poor readers and eight good readers at the six-year-old age
level, and the same numbers at the eight-year-old age level. The children were
from two schools in New Zealand, one just outside a city boundary, and the
other in a suburban area. The children in these schools came from a wide range
of socio-economic backgrounds. All spoke English as their first language. The
reading programmes in these schools encouraged reading for meaning, including
the use of context as a strategy for recognising words (See Appendix to this volume).

The procedure was that half the children read the stories first, before the
lists, while the other half read the lists first, before the stories. To ensure use of
context, children's errors were only counted if they occurred in stories where
reading accuracy was 90–95%.

The results of the study (see Table 2) showed that the younger and poorer
readers improved in context. This was in line with the original Goodman findings. But the older readers did slightly worse. There are two possible explanations for this discrepant result. First, the procedure involved counterbalancing
with random assignment. In other words, half the children read list before context, but the other half read context before list, whereas children in the classic
study only read list before context. Second, this study had analysed the results
for good and poor readers separately, whereas the classic study had averaged all
the data together.

What was important about the study, however, was that it questioned the results of the Goodman (1965) study, even though it had used 'real texts'. While Goodman's data had characterised reading as a linguistic guessing game, involving the use of context, these data implied that older, good readers did not gain from the use of context, at least not when there was some control for order effects. So context effects seemed to occur for younger and poorer readers, but not older, good readers.

In a further replication study, Nicholson, Bailey & McArthur (1991) looked at what would happen if there were some restriction on the reading levels of the children in each group. This was done in order to check whether the Nicholson *et al.* (1988) results applied only to the very good readers, or to above average readers in general.

Again, there were thirty-two pupils in the study. Half the children were six-year-olds; half were eight-year-olds. Within each group, half the children were poor readers, and half were good. In all, there were four equal groups of eight children. The two schools in the study drew from a wide range of socio-economic backgrounds in New Zealand. One school was from a rural area; the other from a city. All children spoke English as their first language.

One difference in this study was that the 'good' readers were selected only if they met two criteria. First, they had to be in the average range or above average on a word recognition test, with an upper limit of one year above average. Second, they had to be clearly above average on an informal prose test. The idea of this restriction was to exclude the very best readers at each age level, and to focus just on the 'above average'. A second difference was that this study used a different set of prose selections for children to read (Department of Education, 1981). A third difference was that the oral reading accuracy criterion, of 90–96%, was applied to both reading of the lists and reading of the stories, whichever was the initial test condition. For example, if the counterbalancing meant that a child read the list first, then the oral reading accuracy criterion was applied to the list. The idea of this restriction was to put children in a situation where the list was not too hard, and then to see how they fared in context.

This time, the results seemed to support the classic study. The poor and 'above average' readers both gained in context. Yet these results were not clear cut. While inspection of the original results for Nicholson *et al.* (1988) showed that the overall pattern of data was much the same, whether children read the story before the list, or vice versa (see Table 3), analysis of the Nicholson *et al.* (1991) data showed that the improvement in context depended on whether children read context first, or list first (see Table 4). When the data were looked at in this way, it turned out that the good readers made more errors in the list when given the list-context order, and more errors in context when given the context-list order. In contrast, poor readers made more errors in the list format, no matter

Table 3 Re-analysis of the Nicholson *et al.* (1988) data on average word errors in list and in story context

Age	Reading level	Order	n	List average	Context average	% gain*
6	poor	LC	4	8.25	5.00	39
		CL	4	6.25	2.00	68
	good	LC	4	8.25	3.00	64
		CL	4	7.00	5.50	21
8	poor	LC	4	13.50	4.50	67
		CL	4	7.50	5.50	27
	good	LC	4	5.50	6.00	−9
		CL	4	6.25	6.50	−4

*Gain was calculated as shown in Table 1.

Table 4 Average word errors in list and in story context (based on Nicholson *et al.*, 1991)

Age	Reading level	Order	n	List average	Context average	% gain*
6	poor	LC	4	4.75	4.50	5
		CL	4	6.25	3.50	44
	good	LC	4	9.25	6.00	35
		CL	4	5.25	5.50	−5
8	poor	LC	4	5.00	3.50	30
		CL	4	8.00	6.00	25
	good	LC	4	6.75	1.75	74
		CL	4	3.00	4.75	−58

*Gain was calculated as shown in Table 1.

whether they read list before context, or context before list. In other words, poor readers were more reliant on context than good readers, since they made gains in context no matter whether they read the list first, or the story first.

To review the argument so far, it seems that poor readers really do use context to help them recognise words. They read words better in context, no matter what. But good readers' use of context is a bit harder to pin down. In Nicholson *et al.* (1988) the six-year-old good readers were better in context, but not the eight-year-old ones. In Nicholson *et al.* (1991), the six- and eight-year-old good readers both gained in list–context, but not in context–list.

Another Replication

The above findings for good readers suggested the need for a larger study, to clarify the general pattern of results obtained in Nicholson *et al.* (1988, 1991), by using a larger sample of children, and a larger corpus of error data. So a further replication study was carried out (Nicholson, 1991). The first experiment in the study involved 100 good, average and poor readers, at six, seven and eight years of age. The children were selected from two suburban schools in New Zealand, with both schools drawing from a wide range of socio-economic backgrounds. The reading programmes of the schools were similar to those of the previous studies. The selection criteria involved no constraints, so that the good readers at each age level really were the best readers in their classes.

The design of the study was similar to the Nicholson *et al.* (1988) replication except that the order of testing was deliberately not counterbalanced. Instead, the children read the text material first, and then the lists of words, that is, context before list. The reasoning behind this decision was that the effect of context would be stringently tested. If context were important, then it would not matter if the children read context before list. Children would still make more mistakes in the list version, since they would not have context clues to help them.

The materials for the study consisted of a range of passages, taken from three different prose reading tests (Department of Education, 1981, 1983, 1985). With such a wide range of reading ability in the sample, the average number of words read by each ability level varied widely, from about 100 words to nearly 1000. The poor readers tended to read the easiest stories, with the least number of words, while the good readers tended to read the harder passages, with the greatest number of words.

Where possible, the children were given passages from the actual story books from which the test material was taken. This made for a more natural reading situation. After reading each story, the children were also asked to retell what had happened, in their own words. These retellings were not a formal part of the study itself, but they encouraged the children to attend to context, rather than read mechanically. In this way, the study encouraged children to read for meaning, that is, to make use of context clues.

Table 5 Experiment 1: Average word errors in list and in story context: Context before list (based on Nicholson, 1991)

Age	Reading level	n	List average	Context average	% gain*
6	poor	11	22.82	11.09	47
	average	10	32.50	19.40	32
	good	11	28.00	31.55	−33
7	poor	12	16.75	8.33	47
	average	11	27.36	17.46	26
	good	11	31.73	38.55	−63
8	poor	11	20.82	12.64	22
	average	11	31.36	32.09	−14
	good	12	25.25	34.67	−40

*See author note at end of chapter.

The results were analysed according to whether the children's oral reading accuracy was in the 90–94% range, the 95–99% range, and the 90–99% range overall. In other words, the results were analysed according to whether children found the passages relatively easy, or relatively difficult. Since the results were similar at each level, only the overall results will be discussed here (see Table 5).

The findings showed the good, average and poor readers made a similar proportion of errors in context, although the better readers usually had to read longer text and make more errors to achieve a similar proportion to the other groups. The most interesting result was that good readers at each age level read better in the list than in context. In other words, for the good readers, the effect of context did not outweigh the practice effect of reading the stories before the lists. This was the opposite of what happened for the poor and average readers, who read words better in context than in list. That is, for the average and poor readers, the context effect outweighed the practice effect.

The second experiment in the study was basically a follow-up, to see whether the results would match the Goodman (1965) study if done in the same way as the original study, that is, if the children read the list first, then the context. It was important to do this follow-up study, to see if the gains in the classic study were due to the order in which children tackled the reading tasks, that is, where they read list first, and then context.

In the second experiment, there were 97 children, with a balance of good,

Table 6 Experiment 2: Average word errors in list and story context: List before context (based on Nicholson, 1991)

Age	Reading level	n	List average	Context average	% gain*
6	poor	5	15.40	4.80	68
	average	8	28.13	8.00	70
	good	14	50.07	35.86	24
7	poor	10	21.10	8.00	58
	average	11	41.00	26.64	34
	good	13	32.77	29.92	17
8	poor	9	19.22	10.00	44
	average	11	26.09	18.64	24
	good	10	27.40	17.90	24

*See author note at end of chapter.

average and poor readers, at six, seven and eight years of age. The children were drawn from one suburban school in a middle-class area. The reading programmes were as in the previous experiment (see Appendix).

The procedures for the second experiment were the same as in the first, that is, the children were asked to read lists of words, straight up and down, but starting from the last word of the story, and ending with the first word. Again, in context, the passages were from the actual storybooks wherever possible, so as to create a natural reading situation. After reading each passage, the child was asked to retell what it was about. The only difference in procedure for the second experiment was that the children were all given the words in list form before reading them in context.

Unfortunately, 6 of the 11 poor readers in the six-year-old group were unable even to read the easiest story, without dropping below the 90% accuracy cut-off point. This reduced the sample to 91. The results were analysed, as in the first experiment, at 90–94, 95–99 and 90–99% accuracy. The general pattern was the same at all levels of accuracy, so only the results for 90–99% accuracy will be discussed here (see Table 6).

The results were in line with the classic study, although the apparent gains in context for the seven- and eight-year-old good readers, and the eight-year-old average readers, were not statistically significant. In short, in this second experiment, the benefits of context went to the poor and average readers, and to the six-year-old good readers rather than to the seven- and eight-year-old good readers.

Reaching a Decision on Context

The research reported in this chapter suggests that the classic study overestimated the positive effects of context. Instead the research dramatically highlights the gap between it, and popular opinion on this topic. Instead of being in line with popular opinion, the research is more in line with Stanovich's (1980) interactive–compensatory model of reading. This model argues that less skilled readers rely on context to compensate for their poor decoding skills, whereas good readers do not need to do so, since they already have good decoding skills.

An example of the compensatory process for one six-year old poor reader is shown below. This child misread a number of words in list form in the Nicholson (1991) study, yet was able to read the same words correctly in context:

List	Child's response
you	why
for	✓
book	dock
good	goed
a	✓
is	✓
it	✓
said	✓
they	✓
too	✓
book	dock
the	✓
like	lik
we	✓

Context

'We like the book too', they said.
'It is a good book for you'.

But does this compensatory process always lead to reading failure? The answer may be as Tunmer (1990) suggests, that the ability to use context at an early stage of reading development, combined with the ability to use letter–sound information, can help children to become sufficiently skilled at decoding so they no longer need to rely on context. In other words, reliance on context can have a positive effect on learning to read if, in the process, children learn to decode. However, if learning to decode does not happen, then children will not learn to read.

Concluding Remarks

In the next chapter, this explanation will be looked at in more detail, as part of a wider discussion of the theoretical debate about how we read, and how children learn to read. So, while the aim of this chapter was to establish the case against context, the next chapter will be more positive. It will look at the practical things that can be done to help all children succeed in learning to read.

Author note

The percentage gains in Tables 5 and 6, taken from Nicholson (1991), were calculated in a different way to Goodman (1965). Instead, the overall gain for each group was calculated by averaging *individual* percentage gains. This is more precise, and necessary for statistical analysis. However, even if the reader were to apply the Goodman (1965) method of calculation, the general pattern of results turns out to be much the same.

References

Adams, M. J. and Huggins, A. W. (1985) The growth of children's sight vocabulary: A quick test with educational and theoretical implications. *Reading Research Quarterly* 20, 262–81.

Allington, R. (1978) Effects of contextual constraints upon rate and accuracy. *Perceptual and Motor Skills* 46, 1318.

Blanchard, J. (1979) Research revisited: A linguistic study of cues and miscues in reading. *Reading Psychology* 1, 66–72.

Department of Education (1981) *An Alternative Informal Prose Reading Test.* Hamilton, New Zealand: Department of Education.

— (1983) *An Informal Reading Test.* Wellington, New Zealand: Department of Education.

— (1985) *Prose Selections.* Wellington, New Zealand:Department of Education.

Goodman, K. S. (1965) A linguistic study of cues and miscues in reading. *Elementary English* 42, 639–43.

— (1987) To my professional friends in Australia and New Zealand. *ARA Today: A Quarterly Newsletter from the Australian Reading Association*, August, p. 6.

Lindfors, J. (1987) *Children's Language and Learning* (rev. edn). Englewood Cliffs, NJ: Prentice Hall.

Negin, G. A. (1981) Students' abilities to recognise words in isolation and in context. *Reading Improvement* 18, 73–80.

Nicholson, T. (1986) Reading is not a guessing game: The great debate revisited. *Reading Psychology* 7, 197–210.

—— (1991) Do children read words better in context or in lists?: A classic study revisited. *Journal of Educational Psychology* 83, 444–50.

Nicholson, T., Bailey, J. and McArthur, J. (1991) Context cues in reading: The gap between research and popular opinion. *Journal of Reading, Writing and Learning Disabilities* 7, 33–41.

Nicholson, T., Lillas, C. and Rzoska, M. A. (1988). Have we been misled by miscues? *The Reading Teacher* 42, 6–10.

Pearson, P. D. (1978) On bridging gaps and spanning chasms. *Curriculum Inquiry* 8, 353–63.

Samuels, S. J. (1985) Word recognition. In H. Singer and R. B. Ruddell (eds) *Theoretical Models and Processes of Reading* (3rd edn) (pp. 256–75). Newark, DE: International Reading Association.

Singer, H. and Ruddell, R. B. (eds) (1985) *Theoretical Models and Processes of Reading* (3rd edn). Newark, DE: International Reading Association.

Staff (1986, August) This week's citation classic. *Current Contents: Social and Behavioral Sciences* 18, 12.

Stanovich, K. E. (1980) Toward an interactive–compensatory model of individual differences in the development of reading fluency. *Reading Research Quarterly* 16, 32–71.

—— (1986) Matthew effects in reading: Some consequences of individual differences in the acquisition of literacy. *Reading Research Quarterly* 21, 360–407.

Stanovich, K. E., Cunningham, A. E. and Feeman, D. J. (1984) Relation between early reading acquisition and word decoding with and without context: A longitudinal study of first grade children. *Journal of Educational Psychology* 76, 668–77.

Tunmer, W. E. (1990) The role of language prediction skills in beginning reading. *New Zealand Journal of Educational Studies* 25, 95–114.

5 Reading Without Context

TOM NICHOLSON

This chapter will consider how children can learn to read without having to use context as a major strategy for recognising words. In doing so, the major models, that is, those of Goodman, Gough, and Stanovich, will be looked at. There will be an analysis of their strengths and weaknesses, as well as their contribution to our understanding of how children learn to read.

The Goodman Model

We start by looking at the Goodman (1970) model. What made it different was the idea of reading as a 'psycholinguistic guessing game', where linguistic guesswork was seen as more important than the graphic information on the page:

> Skill in reading involves not greater precision, but more accurate first guesses based on better sampling techniques, greater control over language structure, broadened experiences and increased conceptual development. As the child develops reading skill and speed, he uses increasingly fewer graphic cues. (p.266)

The strength of the model, also referred to as a top-down model, was its focus on children's reading strategies in text situations. Goodman's analysis of children's errors, or 'miscues', inspired the model, since many errors seemed contextually appropriate. To illustrate this process, imagine the child who misread *sheep* as *lamb*. This child would have made a miscue, according to Goodman, in that context clues were used to facilitate word recognition, and not just visual clues. Again, the child who misread *isn't* as *ain't* would have done the same. According to Goodman & Burke (1973):

> Miscues are generated by the reader in the same way that expected responses are, and with use of the same information. They are miscues in the sense that the reader, in the process of reading, makes a deviation from the path that would lead to the expected response (p. 1).

Another valuable aspect of the Goodman model was that it made specific predictions that could be tested. If a model can be tested, then it is subject to disproof, which means that researchers can challenge the model. If it fails the challenge, then new models can be developed, and the field can advance (Platt, 1964).

One prediction that sprang from the model was that children's errors did not necessarily interfere with comprehension. The logic of the model suggested that good readers would guess, or predict, the meaning of the text, and this would sometimes lead to error, but that this should not cause problems for comprehension. The reasoning was that good readers would read for meaning rather than for precise word identification. For example, what if a child, reading a story, misread the word *toy* as *too*? According to Goodman (1970), the meaning could still be retained:

> Having called (train) *toy*, she calls (*toy*) too (actually it's an airplane in the pictures) not once, but consistently throughout the story. That doesn't seem to make sense. That's what the researcher thought too, until the child spoke of a '*little red too*' later in retelling the story. 'What's a "*little red too*"', asked the researcher. 'An airplane', she replied calmly. So a train is *toy* and a plane is a *too*. Why not? (p.267)

In short, if the Goodman model were correct, then we would expect that good readers would still be able to work out the meanings of words, even if they had misidentified them in text. For example, in a television programme called 'How do you read?' (Rose, 1975), a child misread the word *pheasant* as 'peasonant', while reading a story to Ken Goodman. Later, in reflecting on this miscue, Goodman stated that the child was much too intent on pronouncing the word correctly, instead of reading for meaning. Instead of 'peasonant', Goodman suggested that 'wild turkey' would be more appropriate.

But although such use of context would help the reader to make better sense of the story, how easy is it for children to predict, or guess, the probable meanings of words like 'pheasant'? To find out, I carried out a study where simulated errors were given to good readers, about eight and nine years of age (Nicholson, 1978; Nicholson, Pearson & Dykstra, 1979). The errors were intended to simulate a typical reading situation, where the child makes about five or six errors over a one hundred word text. According to the Goodman model, these good readers should have been able to guess the meanings of the simulated errors.

For example, in the following extract, an abbreviated section from one of the passages given to the children, the task was to replace the words that did not make sense with words that fitted with the meaning of the passage:

Simulated version
Once there was a king. He lived in an old carrot. Outside there lived a door-
bell. Every night he sat in his cave on the hill and roared ...
Correct version
Once there was a king. He lived in an old castle. Outside there lived a drag-
on. Every night he sat in his cave on the hill and roared.

However, the results of my study did not support the Goodman model, at least
not at the literal level of comprehension. For example, when the word *castle* was
replaced by a simulated error such as *carrot*, children had trouble working out
the exact meaning. And they had just as much trouble if the word *tower* replaced
castle, even though this simulated error made sense. Overall, the children were
only able to guess about 27% of the simulated errors. Such results created problems for the Goodman model. Even the sensible embedded errors did not reveal
the actual word, suggesting that guessing at words might well interfere with precise comprehension. In addition, there was a lost opportunity for vocabulary
extension in the sense that guessing did not reveal that the particular word was
castle, given a simulated error such as *tower*, or *carrot*.

Of course, a criticism of the above results would be that the passages, and
the errors, were contrived, and not realistic of the true situation. Yet a follow-up
study of poor readers showed similar results, in that their 'guesses' were also
disruptive of exact comprehension. For example, if the reader said 'skies' for
'sticks', it was difficult to determine the exact word from the following context.

On the positive side, the results also showed that simulated errors did not
interfere with 'gist' comprehension. Children could make specific errors and
lose out at the word level, but not at the discourse level. In short, the Goodman
model seemed to explain children's ability to survive the effects of reading
errors, and still get the gist of the text. Yet the model did not show how children
could make errors while still getting the precise meaning.

So this first prediction was problematic. But the Goodman model also suggested other predictions, namely, that children would read words better in context than in a list, and that good readers would make better use of context than
poor readers. According to Goodman & Burke (1973):

Low proficiency readers are using the same process as high proficiency
readers but less well. They are less efficient because they use more graphic,
syntactic, and semantic information than they need, they have less produc-
tive strategies for using this information, and they are less effective because
they lose more of the potential meaning (Abstract, unpaged).

The problem with these predictions, as has already been discussed in the previous chapter, is that poor readers do not seem to use 'more graphic information

than they need', as suggested above. Instead, it appears that poor readers are less skilled in the ability to use graphic information, and thus have to compensate for this lack of skill by using syntactic and semantic information as much as possible. On the other hand, good readers are less reliant on syntactic and syntactic information than poor readers, and are more proficient in using graphic information (Stanovich, 1980, 1986; Nicholson, 1986; see also the previous chapter).

The Gough Model

What was so interesting about the Gough (1972) model, when it first appeared, was its total contrast to the Goodman model. In fact, Gough depicted the good reader as a fluent decoder who made no use of context at all. Instead, the fluent decoder made use of internalised letter–sound correspondence rules. In learning to read, Gough argued that the child's task was to learn to decode, that is, to convert graphic characters into phonemes, so that the printed form could be mapped to its spoken form. According to Gough (1972):

> The Reader converts characters into systematic phonemes; the child must learn to do so. The Reader knows the rules that relate one set of abstract entities to another; the child does not. The reader is a decoder; the child must become one. (p. 310)

In the Gough model, guessing only occurred when the reading process broke down, that is, when decoding was difficult. By relying on context clues, the child was able to keep the sense of the text, but at the price of being diverted from the difficult task of learning to decode. As Gough (1972) put it:

> The child who would understand (the text) must try to read rapidly, and if he cannot quickly identify a word, he must guess. The result will frequently be an oral reading error ...
> A guess may be a good thing, for it may preserve the integrity of sentence comprehension. But rather than being a sign of normal reading, it indicates the child did not decode the word in question rapidly enough to read normally. The good reader need not guess; the bad should not (p. 317).

The strength of the Gough model, also referred to as a bottom-up model, was that it showed exactly how the good reader might process print without using context. By doing so, the model was able to show the importance of letter–sound correspondences, and why they were difficult for children to acquire. The model also raised a problem for the use of context. It pointed out that guessing would probably be a result of decoding failure. So, rather than a positive sign, the use of context could be a cause for concern.

However Gough (1981) later modified this position, so as to take account of the fact that many reading errors are not just graphemic errors:

> His (Goodman's) insightful observations of oral reading errors (what he terms MISCUES) committed by children ranging from Appalachia to Hawaii have considerably enriched our data base and increased our appreciation of linguistic variation in reading acquisition. Moreover, his crucial observation that many (if not most) children's miscues cannot be attributed to graphemic or visual confusions clearly demonstrates that a model like Gough (1972) does not accurately describe the beginning reader. The child who reads aloud 'Little Miss Muffet sat on a chair' is plainly doing something other than bottom-up processing (p. 93).

And, in a later 'postscript', Gough (1985) declared that his model was wrong about some things, including the value of context. However, while conceding that context could help in recognising words, he argued that it did not usually do so. As he put it 'while highly predictive context can and does facilitate word recognition, proving a strictly "bottom-up" model like mine wrong, most words are not predictable, and so can only be read bottom-up' (p. 688).

The Stanovich Model

In making the above concession, Gough (1985) was also giving ground to the model suggested by Stanovich (1980). The Stanovich model was a variation of the interactive model proposed by Rumelhart (1977). The 'interactive' idea about reading was that normal word recognition made simultaneous use of information from top-down as well as bottom-up processes.

Stanovich added a compensatory mechanism to the interactive model. In other words, Stanovich argued that when bottom-up processes failed, the reader would use top-down processes instead. In the normal situation, however, Stanovich argued that the reading process was bottom-up, and the use of top-down processes only took place in order to compensate for a breakdown in decoding. According to Stanovich (1980):

> The compensatory assumption states that a deficit in any knowledge source results in a heavier reliance on other knowledge sources, regardless of their level in the processing hierarchy. Thus, according to the interactive–compensatory model, the poor reader who has deficient word analysis skills might possibly show a *greater* reliance on contextual factors. In fact, several studies have shown this to be the case (p. 63).

The strength of the Stanovich model was that it helped to explain why poor readers often seemed to make use of context clues in reading. It suggested that contextually appropriate errors occurred when children were unable to use their decoding skills, and had to make use of context. In other words, like the Gough model, this model suggested that the crucial problem facing poor readers was an inability to decode rather than an inability to use context.

Looking back, it may be that Gough (1985) conceded ground to the Stanovich model because it was very similar to his own model. In fact, Gough (1972) had also suggested that guessing was a result of poor decoding. So there was agreement, in the models of both Gough and Stanovich that the hallmark of the good reader was the ability to decode.

Learning to Decode

Interestingly, the term 'decoding' has been used by Goodman as well, but in a very different way. According to Goodman (1970), decoding involved linguistic guesswork, where the reader sampled graphic information, but relied mainly on context clues to recover the meaning of the word. As we have discussed already, Goodman's idea of decoding did not necessarily mean reading the exact word on the page. What mattered was that the meaning was correct. As Goodman (1976) put it, 'the basic decoding is directly from print to meaning' (p. 482).

In New Zealand, this view of decoding seems to have been adopted by the Ministry of Education in its teacher handbook, *Reading in Junior Classes* (Department of Education, 1985):

> Reading may be thought of as a constantly repeated process of sampling, predicting, confirming and self-correcting. At the outset, the text is sampled, and significant visual features are searched for and picked out, some words and/or letters being instantly recognised.
> On this basis, predictions of meaning and text are made. This enlightened guessing makes use of the reader's background experience and oral knowledge, and the semantic, syntactic and grapho-phonic cues which the sampling has brought into focus (p. 25).

Yet looking back over the competing models, such a view of skilled reading seems wrong. The child, according to this model, will rely on context clues to reveal the meanings of words. The problem, as was pointed out in the last chapter, is that this strategy is exactly the one that characterises poor readers.

In contrast, Gough's (1972) view of decoding (see also Gough & Hillinger, 1980; Juel, Griffith & Gough, 1986) is totally different in that it does not involve context at all, except as a back-up. Gough (1972) argued that decoding involved learning how to recode letters into their phonological form. If this could be done, then we could look up words in our mental lexicons, that is, mental dictionaries, in the same way as with spoken words. In short, the advantage of decoding phonologically was that the language system was already well equipped to look up words in this way. However, Gough's (1981) modification of his original position did allow that context would enter the reading process if the decoding process either slowed down or broke down. In addition Gough has also conceded that context can help children to correct a word that has been mispronounced. As Gough & Hillinger (1980) put it, many errors, '(like/ijr/for *eager*) are easily detected and corrected in context' (p. 186).

In fact, there is some research by Groff (1983) to support this view of context as a back-up to decoding. What Groff did was read a little story to children in second grade, where he simulated some phonics-type errors, that is, where irregular words were read as if they were regularly spelled. For example, *have* was read as 'hayve', *head* was read as 'heed', *find* was read as 'finned'. Groff found that only 7% of the children's guesses missed the real word.

However, as Gough & Hillinger (1980) point out, the first step in learning to read is to realise the nature of the alphabetic cipher, and proceed to work it out, that is, 'to break the code' (p. 188). This requires four things. First, the child must learn to recognise the letters of the alphabet. Although some letters look similar (e.g. b, d), children have to learn how to tell them apart. Most children do learn the alphabet, but usually through sheer practice in naming the letters.

Second, the child must be able to identify phonemes in words. This is not the same as knowing that letters have sounds (e.g. b = 'beh'). The phoneme represented by the letter *b* is impossible to say because of the problem of parallel transmission, where information about this particular phoneme is associated with the phonemes that follow it (Matthei & Roeper, 1983). However, despite this difficulty with some letters, quite a few letters have phonemes that are easier to approximate (e.g. m, n, f, s). And, even with difficult letters, such as the letter b, it is still possible to infer the phonemes that are embedded in their sounds (e.g. b in 'beh'). Helping children infer these letter-sound correspondences can also be made easier by using lists of words in which the task is to attend to a particular part of the word, e.g. *bag, bin, bat, but* ... This is not an easy task, since it requires the ability to segment sounds within words, and this appears to be a late-developing skill (see Tunmer, Pratt & Herriman, 1984). However, it is a teachable skill (Bradley & Bryant, 1983; Lundberg, Frost & Petersen, 1988).

If children can learn the alphabet, and the phonemes they represent, then they are in a position to work out how written words can be decoded phonologically. For example, if the child is faced with the unfamiliar written word *fetch*, the task of decoding requires the child to recognise that the five letters represent a series of three phonemes, and that these phonemes are realised as the spoken word 'fetch'. Yet this way of 'decoding' is totally different to the ideas in Goodman's model. For example, here are some extracts from the top-down 'decoding' strategies for reading the word 'fetch', as recommended in *Reading for Junior Classes* (Department of Education, 1985):

- Try reading from the beginning [of the sentence] again, and think what would fit.
- Leave the word out, read on and think about what would make sense. Then come back and see if it fits.
- *Does* that make sense?
- Are you sure?
- What does your word begin with? Is it the same (*as in the text*)?
- Are you happy with that? (pp. 39–40).

As has already been discussed, the above strategies, involving the use of context clues, are common among children, but they are also common among poor readers, suggesting that these are not the crucial skills that distinguish the good reader from the poor. In short, this kind of 'enlightened guessing' (Department of Education, 1985: 25) could not be the full story about how children learn to read.

How then, is bottom-up decoding best acquired? There are two possibilities to consider. The first idea is that children can use the kinds of contextual strategies advocated in *Reading in Junior Classes* (Department of Education, 1985), but use them as a way of learning to decode. The second idea is to teach decoding, directly, without context clues, as in phonics.

This first idea involves using context clues to learn how to decode. Tunmer, Nesdale & Wright (1987) found that six-year-old good readers, matched in reading level with eight-year-old, but poorer readers, showed higher levels of syntactic awareness than the older readers. This finding suggested that it may be important to teach children to use context clues, plus letter–sound information, to guess the forms of unfamiliar words. As they put it, 'with each word correctly identified, the child would increase his/her knowledge of the letter-sound correspondences' (p. 26).

However, this is *not* the same as the 'enlightened guessing', which is used in the top-down approach, for reading words like 'fetch'. As Tunmer (1990) puts it:

> It is important to distinguish this type of contextual facilitation from that associated with the views of Goodman and Smith. Goodman and Smith argue that the use of context to predict words is the major feature of *ongoing* sentence processing, whereas the view proposed here is that the ability

to reflect on sentence structures (i.e. syntactic awareness) *in combination with* emerging phonological recoding skills is essential for *acquiring* word recognition skills. Total or over-reliance on contextual *guessing* to identify unfamiliar words will result in little progress ... (p. 101).

So, for example, if the child were to use letter-sound information plus context, this would enable the child to realise that what seems to be 'wak' is actually 'wake'. Then, next time a similar pattern occurred, say, with words like *joke* or *bake*, where the final *e* signalled a long vowel sound, the child might be able to decode these words correctly, by using letter–sound knowledge. In short, the child does not just sample the print. Instead, the child uses context as a way of acquiring the rules of the alphabetic cipher. According to Tunmer (1990):

> Syntactic awareness may facilitate the development of recoding skill by enabling children to combine knowledge of the constraints of sentential context with incomplete graphophonemic information to identify unfamiliar words. As more words are correctly identified, children's knowledge of the grapheme–phoneme correspondences will increase. This contextual facilitation may be especially important in learning more complex rules, such as those whose application depends on either the position of the letter in the word, or on the presence of a 'marker' letter (p. 101).

The use of context clues and letter–sound information to learn to read irregularly spelled words has also been looked at by Adams & Huggins (1985). They found that proficient readers, that is, children who were good at decoding, were also better at using context to identify irregularly spelled words, like 'ocean' in 'The ship sailed across the ocean'. However, as Gough & Walsh (1991) have shown, the ability to decode irregular, word-specific spellings, like 'shoe' and 'tongue', also depends on mastery of the alphabetic cipher, that is, the set of letter–sound rules which map printed words to their spoken forms. As they put it, 'word-specific knowledge, rather than being deployed in a separate mechanism, is instead gathered within the same mechanism within the cipher'. In short, letter–sound rules can be acquired with the help of context, and these in turn provide the basic mechanism which enables children to read not only regularly spelled words, but irregular ones as well.

Let's now look at the second idea. This would involve teaching children a set of phonics rules, either directly or indirectly, so that they could work out unfamiliar words for themselves. Phonics consists of a set of heuristics for teaching children letter–sound correspondences (e.g. ch is pronounced 'ch'). These rules do not always work, but they certainly highlight the idea of letters corresponding to sounds. However, as Gough (1972) has pointed out, phonics is not the same as phonological recoding. The child who says 'beh-ah-geh' for *bag* is not decoding. Instead, the child is trying to use phonics strategies to approximate how the word is pronounced. But, even if phonics has the simple value of helping children to work out words 'in loco parentis' (Gough, 1972: 312), it certainly approaches more closely to the nature of phonological recoding than does Goodman's view of decoding.

In this respect, the phonics approach used by Calfee and Associates (1981–1984) seems to avoid some of the problems mentioned by Gough, especially in the way it uses lists of examples of the correspondences to be learned. In addition, this approach encourages children to look for patterns and structure while learning letter-sound correspondences. In short, children are taught to think about the correspondences, and to understand how they work. The Calfee *et al.* approach looks at the teaching of vocabulary and comprehension as well as decoding, but we will just look at the decoding part.

An important component of Calfee *et al.*'s phonics approach is the emphasis on simplicity, so that the decoding task is presented in manageable chunks. For example, the letter–sound correspondences of Anglo-Saxon words are learned first, since these words are the 'common' words of English (Calfee & Drum, 1986 — see Table 1). Once these patterns are dealt with, the teacher then moves on to the 'classy' words, borrowed from French, Latin and Greek. These are the words that usually occur in more advanced material, as children move through the higher grades.

Another important feature of this approach is the way children are told the decoding rules explicitly, even though they also learn the rules through implicit examples. This is done by analysing lists of words where the rules follow a 'same' pattern (e.g. bat, hat, mat, fat), a 'same and different' pattern (e.g. hat–hate, can–cane, fad–fade, tap–tape), and a 'mixed' pattern (e.g. bit, rate, note, rat). In the preceding examples, for instance, children are able to study the way in which the final e signals the long vowel sound (Calfee *et al.*, 1981–84 — see Table 2).

These activities certainly encourage the child to think about how the letter–sound correspondences work. And the rules are made simple, in the sense that the lists focus just on one rule at a time. Moreover, the children have to explain, in small group discussion, what is happening in the lists and why the patterns fit with the 'rules'. Such discussion helps the teacher to ensure that the rules are learned properly and are not confused (see Table 3). I have taught these techniques to my students, who have in turn worked with six-, seven-, and eight-year-old children, for the last three years, and have found that this kind of teaching can easily fit within a reading environment in which children do lots of 'real' reading. These ideas are also discussed in Nicholson (1991), and in Henry (1990).

Table 1 The basic structure of letter–sound correspondences in Anglo-Saxon words in English (Calfee & Drum, 1986: 814)

	CONSONANTS	
Single letter	*Blended*	*Digraphs*
Consistent and simple correspondences, easily learned:	Combination of single letter sounds:	Relatively few combinations, each consistent:
b a *t*	*st* a *nd*	*ch* atter
f i *n*	*pr* o *ng*	*sh* are
p i *ll*	*spl* i *nt*	*th* eir, *th* ing
		wh ere

	VOWELS		
Long vs short	*r and l affected*		*Digraphs*
mate mat	par pare pal pall		One sound:
Pete pet	her here —		ai/ay maid, may
pining pinning	sir — —		ee meet
biter bitter	for — —		oa boat
nodes nods	— — —		oi/oy foil, toy
cubed cubbed			au/aw taut, law
			eu/ew feud, few
			Two sounds:
			ea breath breathe
			oo cook food
			ou/ow { round four / cow snow

In short, if phonics is taught systematically and well, so as not to confuse children, it may also facilitate the acquisition of phonological recoding skills, providing of course, that children have the necessary prerequisite skills to profit from such instruction, especially the skills of phonological awareness (Foss & Hakes, 1978; Tunmer & Nesdale, 1985).

Table 2 Examples of the three basic list patterns to illustrate the way the final *e* signals the long vowel sound (Calfee *et al.*, 1981–84)

Same pattern

List 1	List 2
pat	mat
hat	fat
cab	spat
tap	stack
pad	flack
ham	black
fan	stamp

Same and different pattern

List 1	List 2
at	ate
mat	mate
man	mane
mad	made
cap	cape
glad	glade
dam	dame

Mixed pattern

List 1	List 2
fat	fin
fate	fine
cape	cut
cap	cute
mat	not
mate	note
can	kit
cane	kite

Theory and Reality

Before leaving this topic, however, it would be prudent to discuss some of the controversy that surrounds the question of whether or not to teach decoding.

Table 3 An outline of a teaching script which shows the opening, middle and closing of a lesson on short and long vowel patterns. The script also shows how the lesson looks at content (what is studied), process (how it is studied) and structure (the schematic way in which the pattern is studied) (based on Barton & Calfee, 1989).

	Content *(what was learned)*	*Process* *(how it was learned)*	*Structure* *(strategies to learn by)*
Open	Today we are going to study short and long vowel sounds. We'll look at words that have this pattern. We'll also compare these words with other words. This will help you to figure out new words when you read. For example, we will look at words like *mat* and *mate* and talk about the rule which makes us pronounce them in different ways	To study these short and long vowel patterns, we will look at lists of words. Some lists will have the same pattern, but others will have different patterns, and others will have mixed-up patterns.	To help you learn this pattern we'll be using a special way of studying. First, we will read lists where the words look the same. Then, we will read lists where the words look the same but are different. Then, we will read lists where the words are mixed-up. For example: (1) hat, mat = same (2) mat, mate = same/ different (3) hat, hot = mixed
Middle	In this first activity we will look at lists of words where the pattern is either the same, or same and different, or mixed.	How are these words the same? What is the vowel sound? (What clues tell you?) Read the lists. How are they the same? How are they different?	What is the pattern that helps us to know how to pronounce these words? How do the lists help to show the rule?
Close	Let's go over what we studied today. What was the pattern of vowel sounds? What clues helped to separate short and long vowels? What was the main vowel pattern? What other vowels did we study? What were some of the words?	Let's go over how we studied these patterns. What was the first kind of list we studied? What was the other kind of list? How did we find the pattern? This way of looking for patterns will help you when you come to similar words, like *fin* and *fine, dan* and *dane*.	Let's go over the special structure we used to study vowel patterns. First, we looked at a single list of the same pattern. Then we looked at two lists, with patterns that were different. This structure was very helpful to show how the vowel pattern worked.
Follow up to Middle (deep middle)	Let's look at this page from a story and see if we can find more words that fit this pattern	Look at line 3 — can you find a word that fits the pattern? What list can we put this word pattern in?	Can you find some extra words that we could put in a same–different list?

As has already been pointed out, it is wrong to take the extreme position that using context clues is a waste of time. As Tunmer (1990) has put it:

> Although Goodman and Smith are incorrect in arguing that visual information and context free word recognition skills are relatively unimportant in reading, it is possible that some of their recommendations are correct, but for the wrong reasons. (p. 98)

Tunmer's (1990) argument, as discussed already, is that the ability to use context may help children to learn to decode, so that eventually they will not need to rely on context to help with word recognition.

But those who support enlightened guessing tend to be those who see reading as a natural, 'whole-language' activity, and this does not include an emphasis on learning to decode. For example, they are very wary of phonics (see the discussion of phonics in Adams et al., 1991). A complicating factor is that the research on decoding versus whole language is inconclusive. The only major comparison of reading methods was carried out by Bond & Dykstra (1967), some 25 years ago. The report of this study, with its careful statistical analyses, took up an entire issue of *Reading Research Quarterly*. The results of the study showed that code-emphasis approaches tended to be better than approaches which emphasised the use of context clues to recognise words (see also Dykstra, 1968).

However, there may have been other variables that accounted for the good showing of phonics in the Bond & Dykstra study. As Thompson & Johnston (Chapter 3 in this volume) have pointed out:

> Schools which choose to emphasise phonics instruction may have had a higher probability of being schools which have a more than average concern to raise reading standards and have provided more steeply graduated levels of reading instruction which demand faster overall progress in the attainment of students. Any claimed better reading attainment may derive from a number of associated factors, such as this difference in levels of difficulty of instruction provided (or time and resources devoted to the instruction) rather than any specific difference in children's processes of learning (p. 75).

Yet even if there were a lot of support for code-emphasis methods (and there is; see Chall, 1983; Adams, 1990), these methods would still not be accepted by those who see reading as enlightened guessing. As Pearson (1989) has pointed out, talking about 'skills' among whole-language supporters is not a good idea:

> There may even be occasions when whole-language advocates would tolerate a lesson on punctuation or sound-to-letter correspondences; but to utter

phrases such as *skill instruction* or *let's break it down into steps* is to end the conversation (p. 239).

However, to be fair, it should also be said that advocates of phonics have no time for whole-language methods either. In fact, it seems that both groups are at war with each other. According to Pauline Gough (1989), who is not the author of the Gough model, but who edits *Phi Delta Kappan*:

> Two camps of zealots ... have jumped into the fray without even bothering to hear both sides of the debate. Each camp has drawn its wagons into a circle and refused to budge. In such standoffs, there are no winners. And children are the losers (p. 498).

Interestingly, New Zealand is seen as a great success story for the whole-language approach. It is the home of guessing. As Goodman (1987) put it:

> In North America now, in both Canada and the United States, a grass roots whole-language movement is spreading rapidly among teachers. This positive holistic philosophy is strongly rejecting the view that children must first be taught to recode print as sound before they can be permitted to read texts which make sense. These teachers are doing what you in New Zealand have done so successfully with your little books, big books, shared reading and your support of young readers as learners. (p. 6)

However, the reality is that whole-language, with its focus on enlightened guessing, has not solved New Zealand's reading problems, despite Ken Goodman's optimism. There are still children who are having difficulty in learning to read. In 1989, for instance, 25% of six-year olds were in Reading Recovery programmes, where they received individual remedial reading tuition (Boyd & Bennie, 1991). Yet according to Yetta Goodman (in Adams *et al.*, 1991), the Reading Recovery programme, 'was developed for *a small percentage* of children selected from holistic instructional settings where the vast majority of children learn to read without direct intensive phonics' (p. 377, my emphasis).

Clearly, there is some misunderstanding about the overall success of whole-language. The fact that one in four six-year olds have to receive reading help after a year in school is a cause for concern. So perhaps the whole-language approach should be re-evaluated. This approach has been used in New Zealand for more than 25 years, and it may be time to look at other options. One strategy would be to conduct a controlled study in which Tunmer's ideas could be tested, as well as Calfee's ideas on phonics, either as supplements to the whole-language approach, or as separate approaches altogether. In this way, the relative benefits of these ideas, in comparison with whole-language, could be established. Such research should also be considered in other countries as well, where the whole-language approach is emphasised.

Perhaps the best option of all would be to find ways of bringing teachers up to date with current research on this issue, and the political agendas that surround it. Reading is so political, with profits to be made by commercial interests, and with power to be had by those who are 'in' (Johns, 1991). Teachers need to be as much aware of the politics of reading, as they are of the politics of schooling in general.

Conclusion

To conclude, this chapter has looked at the issue of reading without context. There has been a discussion of the major models of reading, those of Goodman, Gough and Stanovich. This discussion has focused on the contrast between Gough and Goodman in their ideas about decoding. It has also concluded that Goodman's ideas are not the whole story, and may even be a misguided story. In particular, it is suggested that children must learn to decode, and that the use of context clues can be part of this process, as long as they are used in a positive way, so as to facilitate the development of phonological recoding skills, that is, bottom-up 'decoding'.

References

Adams, M. J. (1990) *Beginning to Read: Thinking and Learning About Print*. Cambridge, MA: MIT Press.

Adams, M. J., Allington, R. L., Chaney, J. H., Goodman, Y. M., Kapinus, B. A., McGee,L. M., Richgels, D. J., Schwartz, S. J., Shannon, P., Smitten, B. and Williams, J. P. (1991) Beginning to read: A critique by literacy professionals and a response by Marilyn Jager Adams. *The Reading Teacher* 44, 370–87.

Adams, M. J. and Huggins, A. W. (1985) The growth of children's sight vocabulary: A quick test with educational and theoretical implications. *Reading Research Quarterly* 20, 262–81.

Barton, J. and Calfee, R. (1989) Theory becomes practice: One program. In D. Lapp, J. Flood and N. Farnan (eds) *Content Area Reading and Learning* (pp. 366–78). Englewood Cliffs, NJ: Prentice Hall.

Bond, G. L. and Dykstra, R. (1967) The cooperative research program in first-grade reading instruction. *Reading Research Quarterly* 2, 5–142.

Boyd, R. and Bennie, N. (1991) A summary of Reading Recovery data, 1989. *Research and Statistics Division Bulletin* (Ministry of Education, New Zealand) No. 3, May 109–14.

Bradley, L. and Bryant, P. E. (1983) Categorizing sounds and learning to read: A causal connection. *Nature* 301, 419–20.

Calfee, R. C. and Associates (1981–1984) The book: Components of reading instruction. Unpublished manuscript, Stanford University, Stanford.

Calfee, R. C. and Drum, P. (1986) Research on teaching reading. In M. Wittrock (ed) *Handbook of Research on Teaching* (pp. 804–49). New York: MacMillan.

Chall, J. S. (1983) *Learning to Read: The Great Debate*. (Rev. edn). New York: McGraw-Hill.

Department of Education (1985) *Reading in Junior Classes*. Wellington, New Zealand: Department of Education.

Dykstra, R. (1968) The effectiveness of code- and meaning-emphasis beginning reading programs. *The Reading Teacher* 22, 17–23.

Foss, D. and Hakes, D. (1978) *Psycholinguistics: An Introduction to the Psychology of Language*. Englewood Cliffs, NJ: Prentice Hall.

Goodman, K. S. (1970) Reading: A psycholinguistic guessing game. In H. Singer and R. B. Ruddell (eds) *Theoretical Models and Processes of Reading* (pp. 259–71). Newark, DE: International Reading Association.

— (1976) Behind the eye: What happens in reading. In H. Singer and R. B. Ruddell (eds) *Theoretical Models and Processes of Reading* 2nd edn (pp. 470–96). Newark, DE: International Reading Association.

— (1987, August) To my professional friends in Australia and New Zealand. *ARA Today: A Quarterly Newsletter From the Australian Reading Association* p. 6.

Goodman, K. S. and Burke, C. L. (1973) Theoretically based studies of patterns of miscues in oral reading performance (Project No. 9-0375). Washington, DC: US Department of Health, Education and Welfare.

Gough, P. (1989) fon iks wôrz. *Phi Delta Kappan* 70, 498.

Gough, P. B. (1972) One second of reading. *Visible Language* 6, 291–320.

— (1985) One second of reading: Postscript. In H. Singer and R. B. Ruddell (eds) *Theoretical Models and Processes of Reading* 3rd edn (pp. 687–8). Newark, DE: International Reading Association.

Gough, P. B. and Hillinger, M. L. (1980) Learning to read: An unnatural act. *Bulletin of the Orton Society* 30, 179–96.

Gough, P. B. (1981) A comment on Kenneth Goodman. In M. Kamil (ed.) *Directions in Reading: Research and Instruction* (pp. 92–5). Washington, DC: National Reading Conference.

Gough, P. B. and Walsh, M. A. (1991) Chinese, Phoenicians, and the orthographic cipher of English. In S. Brady and D. Shankweiler (eds) *Phonological Processes in Literacy* (pp. 199–209). Hillsdale, NJ: Lawrence Erlbaum.

Groff, P. (1983) A test of the utility of phonics rules. *Reading Psychology* 4, 217–25.

Henry, M. (1990) *Words: Integrated Decoding and Spelling Instruction Based on Word Origin and Word Structure*. Los Gatos, CA: Lex Press.

Johns, J. L. (1991) Helping readers at risk: Beyond whole-language, whole-word, and-phonics. *Journal of Reading, Writing and Learning Disabilities* 7, 59–68.

Juel, C., Griffith, P. L. and Gough, P. B. (1986) Acquisition of literacy: A longitudinal study of children in the first and second grade. *Journal of Educational Psychology* 78, 243–55.

Lundberg, I., Frost, J. and Petersen, O. (1988) Effects of an extensive program for stimulating phonological awareness in preschool children. *Reading Research Quarterly* 23, 263–84.

Matthei, E. and Roeper, T. (1983) *Producing and Understanding Speech*. Suffolk:Fontana.

Nicholson, T. (1978) The relative effects of different error types on children's understanding of connected discourse (abstracted). *Reading Research Quarterly* 14, 259–64.

— (1986) Reading is not a guessing game: The great debate revisited. *Reading Psychology* 7, 197–210.

— (1991) *Overcoming the Matthew Effect in Reading: Solving Reading Problems*

Across the Curriculum. Wellington, New Zealand: New Zealand Council for Educational Research.

Nicholson, T., Pearson, P. D. and Dykstra, R. (1979) Effects of embedded anomalies and oral reading errors on children's understanding of stories. *Journal of Reading Behavior* 11, 339–54.

Pearson, P. D. (1989) Commentary: Reading the whole-language movement. *Elementary School Journal* 90, 232–41.

Platt, J. R. (1964) Strong inference. *Science* 146, 347–52.

Rose, S. (Producer) (1975) *How Do You Read?* (Film). London: BBC 'Horizon'.

Rumelhart, D. E. (1977) Toward an interactive model of reading. In S. Dornic (ed.) *Attention and Performance VI* (pp. 573–603). Hillsdale, NJ: Erlbaum.

Stanovich, K. E. (1980) Toward an interactive–compensatory model of individual differences in the development of reading fluency. *Reading Research Quarterly* 16, 32–71.

— (1986) Matthew effects in reading: Some consequences ofindividual differences in the acquisition of literacy. *Reading Research Quarterly* 21, 360–407.

Tunmer, W. E. (1990) The role of language prediction skills in beginning reading. *New Zealand Journal of Educational Studies* 25, 95–114.

Tunmer, W. E. and Nesdale A. R. (1985) Phonemic segmentation skill and beginning reading. *Journal of Educational Psychology* 77, 417–27.

Tunmer, W. E., Nesdale, A. R. and Wright, A. D. (1987) Syntactic awareness and reading acquisition. *British Journal of Developmental Psychology* 5, 25–34.

Tunmer, W. E., Pratt, C. and Herriman, M. L. (eds) (1984) *Metalinguistic Awareness in Children: Theory, Research, and Implications.* Berlin: Springer-Verlag.

6 Language-related Factors as Sources of Individual Differences in the Development of Word Recognition Skills

WILLIAM E. TUNMER AND WESLEY A. HOOVER

Introduction

A model of the proximal causes of reading performance differences referred to as the *simple view of reading* proposes that individual differences in reading comprehension are a function of two factors, word recognition and linguistic comprehension, each of which is assumed to be necessary for reading (Gough & Tunmer, 1986; Hoover & Gough, 1990; Hoover & Tunmer, this volume; Juel, Griffith & Gough, 1986; Tunmer & Hoover, 1992). Stated simply, if beginning readers do not understand the language being read, they will have trouble understanding the text. Similarly, if beginning readers cannot recognise the words of text, they will again experience difficulty in understanding the text. Theoretical arguments and empirical evidence in support of this model are presented in the chapter by Hoover & Tunmer (this volume).

If word recognition and linguistic comprehension are indeed the proximal causes of individual differences in reading comprehension performance, what factors contribute to differences in these two variables? In this chapter we examine four different accounts of the role of language-related factors in the development of word recognition skills. Each of these accounts assumes that an essential aspect of the development of word recognition skills is phonological recoding ability, which is the ability to translate letters and letter patterns into phonological forms. Beginning readers must eventually learn to make use of the systematic correspondences between elements of written and spoken language to

123

advance beyond an initial stage of reading in which words are recognised by selective association, the pairing of a partial stimulus cue to a response (Byrne, 1991, 1992; Byrne & Fielding-Barnsley, 1989; Gough & Hillinger, 1980; Gough & Juel, 1991; Gough, Juel & Roper-Schneider, 1983). Research on the specific mechanisms by which beginning readers induce sublexical relations is presented in Chapter 2 by Thompson & Fletcher-Finn (this volume).

Each account also assumes that the ability to perform *metalinguistic* operations is essential for acquiring basic reading skills. The task facing beginning readers is to learn to identify unfamiliar words in connected text. In most reading programmes students are taught two general learning strategies: to use graphophonemic cues and to use sentence context cues. (The relative emphasis placed on each of these strategies is a crucial issue; see Chapters 4 and 5 in this volume for further discussion.) The acquisition of these two learning strategies depends on the development of two types of metalinguistic ability, where *metalinguistic ability* (or awareness) is defined as the ability to reflect on and manipulate the structural features of spoken language (Tunmer & Herriman, 1984). To use sentence context cues requires the ability to reflect on the internal syntactic/semantic structure of sentences (called *syntactic awareness*), and to discover correspondences between graphemes and phonemes requires the ability to decompose spoken words into their constituent phonemic elements (called *phonological awareness*).

General Language Ability

According to this view metalinguistic ability develops concomitantly with general language ability (Bowey, 1990). Such an account, argues Bowey (1990), 'provides a framework for integrating research on the association between metalinguistic development and early reading with the findings that individual differences in general language proficiency can predict subsequent reading difficulties' (p. 440). As evidence in support of this view Bowey (1990) cites the results of an earlier study of hers (Bowey & Patel, 1988) which showed that metalinguistic ability (as measured by phonological and syntactic awareness tasks) did not make an independent contribution to variation in the reading comprehension performance of beginning readers, whereas general language ability (as measured by hearing vocabulary and sentence imitation tasks) did. Neither metalinguistic ability nor general language ability made an independent contribution to variation in word decoding. All measures were taken concurrently.

There are several difficulties with the arguments and evidence that Bowey (1990) advances in support of her proposed framework. First, there are independent theoretical reasons for expecting the relationship between general language ability and beginning reading comprehension performance to be stronger than the relationship between metalinguistic ability and reading comprehension performance. According to the simple view of reading discussed earlier, linguistic comprehension is one of two *proximal* causes of individual differences in reading comprehension performance. No matter how proficient children may be at decoding words, their ability to comprehend text will never *exceed* their general language ability. It is for this reason that the strength of the relationship between listening and reading comprehension ability has been found to increase at increasing levels of decoding skill (Hoover & Gough, 1990). Contrary to what Bowey (1990) claims, the fact that metalinguistic ability fails to make an independent contribution to reading comprehension performance when general language ability is included in the regression equation does not provide evidence against the claim that metalinguistic ability is a developmentally distinct kind of linguistic functioning.

Although Bowey & Patel (1988) also found that metalinguistic ability was not related to word decoding when the effects of general language ability were statistically controlled, this finding conflicts with the results of longitudinal studies that have reported significant relationships between metalinguistic ability and later word decoding skills even when the effects of general language and cognitive abilities were held constant (Bryant, MacLean & Bradley, 1990; Tunmer, 1989). An important feature of Bowey's (1990) framework is that it assumes that general language ability is related to word decoding as a consequence of its influence on the development of metalinguistic ability. This would then provide an overall account of the findings that metalinguistic development is related to early reading and that individual differences in general language proficiency predict subsequent reading difficulties. However, Bowey's (1990) account overlooks the possibility that individual differences in general language ability may *directly* influence the development of word decoding skills, irrespective of differences in metalinguistic ability.

For example, children who are unable to discriminate easily between different speech sounds (perhaps because of a history of recurrent otitis media) will likely encounter difficulty in segmenting speech, which, in turn, will hamper the development of their phonological recoding skill (Morais, 1991). Relatedly, children with deficient morphophonemic rule knowledge will be disadvantaged in using this knowledge to break the orthographic code of an alphabetic writing system such as English. For example, the letter *s* represents the regular noun plural inflection, even though it is not always realised as the /s/ phoneme, as is true of words like *dogs* and *cars*, in which the final sound is /z/. However, for beginning readers with morphophonemic rule knowledge it is not necessary to learn the exceptions on a case-by-case basis. In acquiring spoken English, these children unconsciously learn a phonological rule that specifies that the plural inflection is realised as /s/ when it follows a voiceless stop consonant, as in *cats*, and as /z/ when it follows a voiced phoneme, as in *dogs*. When children with such knowledge confront an unfamiliar word, such as the nonsense word spelled *z-o-g-s*, they automatically know that it is pronounced /zogz/, not /zogs/.

Poorly developed lexical representations will also limit the development of children's decoding skills. When beginning readers apply their incomplete knowledge of grapheme–phoneme correspondences to unfamiliar words (including irregular ones), the result will often be close enough to the correct phonological form that they can correctly identify the word and thus increase both their word-specific knowledge and their knowledge of grapheme-phoneme correspondences. However, this can occur only if the unfamiliar word is in their *listening* vocabulary (for related arguments and supportive evidence, see Vellutino & Denckla, 1991; Vellutino & Scanlon, 1987a, 1987b).

Deficiencies in syntactic knowledge may also impair the development of decoding skills by limiting beginning readers' ability to use sentence context as an aid to word identification (Vellutino & Denckla, 1991; Vellutino & Scanlon, 1987a, 1987b). Syntactic knowledge enables beginning readers to monitor accuracy in word identification by providing them with immediate feedback when their responses to the words of text fail to conform to the surrounding grammatical context (such as when their attempted response results in either a violation of a strict sub-categorisation rule, which governs the syntactic structures into which a word can enter, or a violation of a selectional restriction rule, which places constraints on how words of different form classes can be combined). Beginning readers may also combine knowledge of the constraints of sentence context with incomplete graphophonemic information to identify unfamiliar words (which further increases their knowledge of grapheme-phoneme correspondences) and to discover homographic spelling patterns (letter sequences that have different pronunciations in different words, e.g. *own*, as in *clown* and *blown*; and *ear*, as in *bear* and *clear*).

Bowey's (1990) claim that metalinguistic ability develops concomitantly with general language ability fails to explain the great individual differences in metalinguistic abilities observed among children during the early stages of middle childhood, differences which contrast markedly with the relative consistency with which children of this age perform primary linguistic activities (Tunmer & Herriman, 1984). Many four- and five-year-old children who appear to possess normal language comprehension and speaking skills are unable to perform such seemingly simple metalinguistic operations as counting the number of phonemes in words, identifying words that do not rhyme with other words, or correcting word order violations in simple sentence structures (see Tunmer, Pratt & Herriman, 1984, for reviews of research on the development of metalinguistic abilities in children). The ability to perform metalinguistic operations does not come free with the acquisition of language (Shankweiler & Crain, 1986).

Specific Environmental Experiences

Bowey (1990) acknowledges that specific environmental experiences or types of literacy instruction may be required for the development of metalinguistic ability. The environmental view proposes that inadequate exposure to print-related activities prior to schooling and inadequate instruction during schooling are responsible for differences in early reading. A leading proponent of this view is Ehri (1984, 1986, 1987, 1989). She argues that children who are exposed to instruction in letter names/sounds and spelling are able to use their developing knowledge of letters and printed words as mediators in conceptualising separate phonemes and words. This, in turn, enables them to acquire basic decoding skills. Ehri (1989) rejects the view that the phonological deficits of poor readers are the result of more basic phonological deficiencies that existed in the children before reading instruction began (see next section). Rather, she maintains that it is instruction that fails to provide beginning readers with full knowledge of the spelling system that is responsible for limited reading and spelling development and limited phonological awarenes.

According to this view, then, orthographic knowledge is essential for children to be able to manipulate aspects of speech. This suggests that phonological awareness is a *consequence* of exposure to print, a view that would appear to conflict with the widely held view that deficient phonological awareness is a major cause of reading disability (see Tunmer & Rohl, 1991, for a review of research). Evidence consistent with the environmental view comes from studies showing that orthographic knowledge influences children's performance on phonemic segmentation tasks. Tunmer & Nesdale (1982, 1985) found that in a phoneme-counting task beginning readers were much more likely to make over-shoot errors (i.e. errors in which the response given exceeds the number of phonemes in the item) on orally presented words containing digraphs (letter pairs that represent single phonemes, e.g. *sh, oo*) than on similar words not containing digraphs. Similarly, Ehri & Wilce (1980) found that fourth-grade children were more likely to make overshoot errors on a word like *pitch* than on the matched control word *rich*.

Ehri (1989) discounts findings from studies showing that training in phonological awareness produces significant experimental group advantages in reading achievement because, she maintains, such training was combined with *spelling* training that teaches learners how to symbolise sounds with letters. For example, in the frequently cited study by Bradley & Bryant (1985), the group of children that received training in *both* sound categorisation and spelling with plastic letters outperformed the control group on tests of reading and spelling achievement, whereas the group that received training only in sound categorisation failed to show significant gains over the control group. It cannot be determined from this study whether a group that received training only in spelling with plastic letters would have made gains comparable to that of the group that received training in both sound categorisation and spelling.

Longitudinal studies have shown that phonological awareness in children prior to school entry is related to later reading achievement even when children showing any preschool reading ability are excluded (Bradley & Bryant, 1985; Tunmer, Herriman & Nesdale, 1988), or when the influence of preschool reading ability is statistically controlled (Vellutino & Scanlon, 1987b). However, Ehri (1989) points out that preliterate children may nevertheless possess substantial knowledge of letter names and sounds, knowledge which may enable them to acquire rudimentary phonological awareness skills. Prior to school entry children may be exposed to activities in the home that lead to the development of preliterate phonological awareness. These activities may include looking at books and playing games that increase knowledge of letter names and their relation to sounds in words (e.g. 'Z is for Zebra'), playing rhyming and sound analysis games that increase phonological sensitivity, and manipulating movable letters to form pre-conventional spellings of words (e.g. *FRE* for fairy). Ehri (1989) suggests that these 'informal experiences with print … may account for the variation in phonemic awareness scores observed among pre-readers before they begin kindergarten' (p. 363).

Ehri (1986) also discounts findings from studies employing reading-age match designs which show that young, normal readers perform better than older, poor readers on measures of phonological awareness (e.g. Bradley & Bryant, 1978). She cites research indicating that as reading disabled children grow older, their spelling age falls increasingly behind their reading age. This means that if normal and backward readers are matched on reading age, the backward readers will be behind the normal readers in spelling ability. Thus, argues Ehri (1986), 'dyslexics may exhibit phonological deficits because they have not advanced as far in acquiring working knowledge of the orthographic system as a map for speech' (p. 173).

To investigate this claim, Rohl & Tunmer (1988) used a spelling-age match design to determine whether deficits in phonologically-related skills were related to difficulties in acquiring basic spelling knowledge. Poor fifth-grade spellers, average third-grade spellers, and good second-grade spellers matched on a standardised spelling test, and a group of good fifth-grade spellers matched by chronological age with the poor fifth-grade spellers, were administered a phoneme segmentation test containing non-digraph pseudowords and an experimental spelling test containing four types of words (exception, ambiguous, regular and pseudowords). In support of their hypothesis, Rohl & Tunmer (1988) found that when compared with the poor fifth-grade spellers, the average third-grade and good second-grade spellers performed significantly better on the phonological awareness test, made fewer errors in spelling pseudowords, and made spelling errors that were more phonetically accurate. When percentage of orthographically legal misspellings to total errors was the dependent variable, there were no significant differences between the three spelling-matched groups. All three groups performed well, suggesting that even the poor spellers were familiar with legal English letter sequences. Their errors, which were poor phonetic representations of the target words, conformed reasonably well to rules about how letters can be combined, thus emphasising the specific phonological problems of these children. These findings appear to contradict Ehri's view that it is lack of orthographic knowledge per se that causes deficits in phonological awareness and related skills.

In support of this conclusion are the results of a training study by Lundberg, Frost & Petersen (1988) indicating that exposure to print is not a *necessary* condition for the development of phonological awareness, as Ehri (1989) seems to claim. They found that preliterate children with very limited letter-name knowledge could be successfully trained in phonological awareness skills during their kindergarten year without the use of letters. These children and a matched control group were given spelling and reading tests in first and second grade. The training group outperformed the control group only in spelling in first grade, but in both spelling and reading in second grade. Because phonemic segmentation ability has been shown to influence reading achievement through phonological recoding skill (Juel, Griffith & Gough, 1986; Stanovich, Cunningham & Feeman, 1984; Tunmer, 1989; Tunmer & Nesdale, 1985), it is possible that differences in reading performance would have been obtained in first grade if a measure of phonological recoding had been used. This seems especially likely in view of Jorm, Share, MacLean & Matthews (1984) finding that differences in phonological recoding ability at the end of the first year of reading instruction gave rise to steadily increasing differences in future reading achievement even when sight word vocabulary and verbal intelligence at the end of the first year were held constant.

The results of training studies also indicate that knowledge of letter names and/or sounds is not a *sufficient* condition for the development of phonological awareness. Byrne & Fielding-Barnsley (1989) reported that preschool children with no knowledge of reading or the sounds of individual letters were able to achieve criterion performance on a word learning task *only* when letter–sound training was accompanied by training in phonemic segmentation. On the basis of this finding Byrne (1991) concluded that 'learning the sounds that the letters represent is not sufficient ... It needs to be supplemented by appropriate insights into segment separability and segment identity' (p. 83).

This finding was recently confirmed in a training study by Ball & Blackman (1991). Two groups of kindergarten children received training in letter names and letter sounds but only one of these groups received training in phonological awareness as well. Results indicated that only the children in the group that received phonological awareness instruction showed significant gains over a control group in spelling and reading performance, and phonemic segmentation skill. The group that received instruction in letter names and letter sounds alone did not differ from the control group on post-test measures of reading, spelling and phoneme segmentation.

In summary, contrary to Ehri's (1989) views, it appears that knowledge of letter names and/or sounds is neither necessary for acquiring phonological awareness (as demonstrated by the training study of Lundberg, Frost & Petersen, 1988) nor is it sufficient (as demonstrated by the training studies by Ball & Blackman, 1991; Byrne & Fielding-Barnsley, 1989). On logical grounds alone it would appear that at least some minimal level of phonemic segmentation ability is necessary for children to take advantage of letter–name and letter–sound knowledge in learning to read. Whether children learn to associate the name 'dee' or the sound 'duh' with the letter *d*, they must still be able to segment the name or sound to make the connection between the letter *d* and the corresponding abstract phoneme /d/, which cannot be pronounced in isolation.

The likelihood that some minimal level of phonemic segmentation ability is necessary for learning to read does not preclude the possibility that some skills that are acquired or improved as a result of learning to read and spell may greatly improve performance on phonological awareness tasks (Tunmer & Rohl, 1991). Some of these spinoff skills, which include the ability to maintain and operate on verbal material in working memory, to generate orthographic images, and to make use of phoneme-to-letter correspondences, may even be necessary to perform more advanced phonological awareness tasks.

The assumption of a reciprocal relationship between phonological awareness and learning to read would explain why children who have acquired basic reading skills tend to make overshoot errors on phonemic segmentation test items containing digraphs or silent letters (see earlier discussion). The children appear to segment on the basis of the number of letters in the word, or on the number of letters and letter groupings in the word that they believe (perhaps mistakenly) represent individual phonemes in the corresponding spoken word. The assumption of reciprocal causation would also explain why beginning readers (Yopp, 1988), illiterate adults (Morais, Cary, Alegria & Bertelson, 1979), and adults literate only in non-alphabetic orthographies (Read, Zhang, Nie & Ding, 1986) are unable to perform well on phonological awareness tasks that draw heavily on the spinoff skills of reading, such as the phoneme reversal task (say pat backwards) and the phoneme deletion task (say *skip* without the *kuh* sound). Such tasks may amount to little more than indirect measures of reading achievement (Tunmer, 1991; Tunmer & Rohl, 1991).

Although Ehri (1989) appears to be incorrect in suggesting that orthographic knowledge is necessary for children to acquire phonemic segmentation ability, she may nevertheless be correct in arguing that phonological awareness develops mostly during the course of learning to read, and that phonological awareness is not a prerequisite for deriving benefit from beginning reading instruction. Supporting the latter claim are results from a longitudinal study by Tunmer, Herriman & Nesdale (1988). They found that many preliterate 5-year-old children who performed very poorly on a phoneme segmentation task at the beginning of the first year of reading instruction showed average to above average performance on phoneme segmentation and pseudoword decoding tasks at the end of the school year. Despite this finding, however, a contingency analysis of the data at the end of the year indicated that a minimal level of phonological awareness is necessary for acquiring basic phonological recoding skills (as measured by pseudoword decoding). Although many children performed well on phoneme segmentation but poorly on pseudoword decoding, no children performed poorly on phoneme segmentation but well on pseudoword decoding. Thus, the claim that phonological awareness is not a cognitive prerequisite for taking advantage of reading *instruction* is not inconsistent with the claim that phonological awareness is a cognitive prerequisite for reading *acquisition*. As Stanovich (1989) points out in a commentary on Ehri's (1989) paper, the key question is what causes differences in individual *responsiveness* to instructional activities, both formal and informal? The views described in the next two sections attempt to address this issue.

Phonological Processing in Working Memory

According to this view differences in the ability to acquire basic word decoding skills are the result of differences in the ability to maintain and operate on phonological material in working memory (Brady & Fowler, 1988; Liberman & Shankweiler, 1985, 1991; Liberman, Shankweiler & Liberman, 1989; Mann, 1987; Mann, Cowin & Schoenheimer, 1989; Shankweiler & Crain, 1986; Stanovich, 1987, 1988a, 1988b, 1991). A deficient language module is assumed to be responsible for limitations on the use of phonological structures in working memory. Evidence in support of this view comes from studies showing that poor readers are deficient in their ability to maintain a phonological code in working memory (for reviews of research see Liberman & Shankweiler, 1985; Liberman, Shankweiler & Liberman, 1989; Mann, 1986; Mann, Cowin & Schoenheimer, 1989; Shankweiler & Crain, 1986). They perform less well than normal readers in tasks requiring the ordered recall of strings of digits, letters, nameable objects, nonsense syllables, or words. In addition, they are less sensitive to phonologically confusable items in recall tasks. These deficiencies appear to be limited to the language domain, since other kinds of materials, such as nonsense designs and faces, can generally be retained in working memory without deficit by poor readers.

Deficiences in the ability to retain phonological information in working memory could interfere with the development of word decoding skills in at least three ways. Firstly, because English orthography is primarily a system for relating phonemes to patterns of graphemes co-occurring within words, and because there is no one-to-one correspondence between phonemes and segments of the acoustic signal, it is not possible to directly teach children individual grapheme-phoneme correspondences. Children must therefore discover the correspondences by reflecting upon the elements of written and spoken *words*. As Gough & Hillinger (1980) argue, 'the crucial learning event occurs when the child perceives (or thinks of) a printed word at the same time he perceives (or thinks of) its spoken counterpart' (p. 192). This, of course, requires the ability to maintain phonological material in working memory.

Second, beginning readers who rely on 'sounding out' strategies in identifying unfamiliar words must perform blending operations that require serial processing of isolated sounds (e.g. *buh ah guh* for the printed word *bag*). Each non-continuant sound must be segmented to isolate the initial phoneme, which is then stored in working memory while the next sound is 'cleaned up' (Perfetti, Beck, Bell & Hughes, 1987). The phonemes held in memory are then combined to form a candidate word, which is then compared with word candidates from the mental lexicon. The process of performing blending operations clearly places great demands on working memory. In support of this claim, positive correlations have been reported between blending ability and performance on short-term memory tasks (Wagner *et al.*, 1987).

Third, sentence context that is stored in working memory can be used to facilitate word identification. As noted earlier, the constraints of sentence context enable beginning readers to monitor accuracy in word identification by providing them with feedback when their responses fail to conform to the surrounding grammatical context. In addition, beginning readers can combine sentence context information with (possibly incomplete) knowledge of grapheme-phoneme correspondences to identify unfamiliar regular and irregular words, which further increases their knowledge of grapheme-phoneme correspondences. Deficient working memory ability could prevent readers from taking full advantage of sentence context as an aid to word identification.

Despite the arguments and evidence in support of the verbal working memory deficit hypothesis, there are major difficulties with this view. Much of the evidence cited in support of this account of beginning reading differences is based on studies comparing good and poor readers of similar age and intelligence. A problem with this type of design is that it yields uninterpretable results when a difference in some reading-related variable is found (Bryant, 1986; Bryant & Bradley, 1985). The difference observed between good and poor readers could be either a cause or consequence of reading failure.

This is an important consideration in relation to Matthew effects, or rich-get-richer and poor-get-poorer effects, in reading achievement (Stanovich, 1986). Because of their deficient word recognition skills, poor readers receive much less practice in reading than normal readers. They are thus prevented from taking full advantage of the 'bootstrapping' relationships between reading and other aspects of development, such as vocabulary growth, ability to comprehend more syntactically complex sentences, and development of richer and more elaborated knowledge bases, all of which facilitate *further* growth in reading by enabling readers to cope with more difficult textual materials. Good readers, however, are able to take advantage of the reciprocally facilitating relationships between reading and other reading-related skills (e.g. phonological awareness, phonological recoding) and are therefore able to progress at a faster rate. As a consequence, they read much more than poor readers and receive larger amounts of practice in reading and processing verbal material. In support of this claim, research indicates that large differences between good and poor readers in exposure to print begin to emerge as early as the first year of formal instruction (see Stanovich, 1986, for a review of research).

This additional reading experience may improve the efficiency of phonological processing in working memory in a number of ways. For example, it has been found that idea units in written language are significantly longer and more syntactically complex than those of spoken language (Chafe, 1985). Such linguistic devices as nominalisation, subordination, and modification are used to pack many idea units into a single sentence. Since better readers are exposed to more written language, and more linguistically advanced written language, than poor readers, they receive more practice in maintaining complex linguistic structures in working memory, a possible consequence of which is an improvement in their ability to make effective use of phonological representations in working memory.

As noted earlier, deficiences in the ability to retain phonological information in working memory may hinder the development of word decoding skills in several ways. However, given the nature of Matthew effects, the suggested cause and effect relationship may go in the opposite direction. Blending operations, for example, place a considerable load on verbal working memory. Because better readers read more than poor readers, they receive more practice in performing blending operations, a likely consequence of which is an improvement in their ability to maintain and operate on verbal material in working memory.

Metalinguistic operations may also stress verbal working memory. The ability to analyse the internal structure of spoken words enables children to discover how phonemes are related to graphemes, and the ability to reflect on sentence structures in order to combine knowledge of the constraints of sentence context with incomplete graphophonemic information helps children to identify unfamiliar words, and thus increase both their word specific knowledge and their knowledge of grapheme–phoneme correspondences. It is possible that repeated occurrences of reflecting on spoken words and sentence structures to discover grapheme–phoneme correspondences improves children's ability to maintain a phonological code in memory. That is, improved efficiency in verbal working memory may be a spin-off effect of the metalinguistic operations that children must perform to become skilled readers.

There is considerable evidence in support of these suggestions. Studies employing reading-age match, rather than mental-age match, designs have failed to show differences between good and poor readers in either short-term verbal recall or phonological confusability (Bisanz, Das & Mancini, 1984; Hulme, 1981; Johnston, 1982; Johnston, Rugg & Scott, 1987). The major advantage of the reading-age match design over the mental-age match design is that, because reading levels are the same, it reduces the possibility that any differences that emerge between good and poor readers are merely the product of reading level differences. The results of studies employing the reading-age match design indicate that the phonological coding processes in working memory of older, disabled readers are comparable to those of younger, normal readers of similar reading level.

Several investigators have found a significant relationship between short-term verbal recall in kindergarten and reading achievement in first grade (Mann, 1984; Mann & Liberman, 1984; Share, Jorm, MacLean & Matthews, 1984). However, because these studies failed to control for reading skill in kindergarten, it cannot be concluded that efficiency of phonological coding in working memory is causally related to the acquisition of reading skills. If, as suggested earlier, the process of learning to read itself is largely responsible for the development of verbal working memory, then children who possess some reading ability at school entry would be expected to perform better on short-term verbal recall tasks than children with no reading ability. Preschool reading ability might therefore produce a spurious correlation between preschool verbal working memory ability and later reading achievement.

In support of this suggestion are the results of longitudinal studies in which children showing any preschool reading ability were excluded. Bradley & Bryant (1985), for example, gave a short-term verbal recall task to a group of pre-readers who were four or five years old. Eighteen months later the children were given tests of reading and spelling ability. Bradley & Bryant found that preschool performance on the recall task was not related to later reading achievement. However, they did find a significant relationship between reading ability at age seven and verbal working memory ability (as measured by a test of memory for words) when the children were eight or nine years of age.

In a longitudinal study Ellis & Large (1987) monitored children's performance on several variables (including auditory short-term memory and reading) as they developed from five to seven years of age. To analyse their data they divided the children into three groups based on their IQ and reading scores at age seven: high IQ/low reading, high IQ/high reading, and low IQ/low reading. At age five the two high IQ groups performed at approximately the same level on an auditory word span task, whereas the low IQ/low reading group performed at a below average level. Over the three year period the relative performance of the high IQ/high reading group gradually increased, whereas the relative performance of the low IQ/low reading group remained constant. Most importantly, the relative performance of the high IQ/low reading group steadily declined over the three year period to a level that was similar to that of the low IQ/low reading group. These results strongly suggest that the development of verbal working memory is tied to learning to read.

In a later study Ellis (1990) used LISREL analyses to examine further the relationship between verbal working memory development and learning to read. Because the children in the study were tested on reading and verbal working memory ability at several points, Ellis was able to make cross-lag comparisons of LISREL path co-efficients at two developmental stages: from age five to six years and from age six to seven years. Ellis summarises his findings as follows:

> At each of the two developmental stages Reading skill contributes more to later proficiency in Auditory STM (0.31, 0.36) than the reverse (0.06, 0.18). Indeed Reading is the *best* predictor of Auditory STM at 6 years old (0.31), better than prior levels of Auditory STM itself (0.21) (p. 117).

These results led Ellis (1990) to conclude that 'the acquisition of reading skills makes relevant active phonological processing in short-term memory and thus stimulates the development of these skills' (p. 107).

Further evidence that the development of verbal working memory ability during the school years is largely a consequence of reading development comes from a series of experiments conducted by Torgesen and colleagues (see

Torgesen, 1988). Torgesen was interested in comparing the processing deficiences of two groups of learning disabled children, those who did not have
memory span difficulties (LD-N) and those with severe problems in the short-
term retention of information (LD-S). The children were between nine and
eleven years of age. Torgesen presented several kinds of evidence in support of
the hypothesis that LD-S children are deficient in their ability to process phonological information in working memory. First, the LD-S children did not show a
performance deficit when asked to recall sequences of visual figures that were
difficult to label verbally. Second, performance differences between the LD-S
children and the LD-N children (and a control group of normal children) were
greater when less familiar verbal items were used. Third, performance differences between the LD-S children and other groups decreased when phonologically confusable items were used.

Although these findings are *consistent* with Torgesen's (1988) claim that 'the
performance problems of LD-S children on memory span tasks are caused by difficulties utilising verbal/phonological codes to store information' (p. 608, emphasis
added), the results could also be related to reading ability differences between the
LD-S and LD-N children. Torgesen's data show just that. The two groups performed at a similar level on a standardised test of math achievement. However, the
LD-S children were one grade level behind the LD-N children in reading achievement. Torgesen argues that 'the children with LD in each group were not selected
because of one type of academic disability or another, so the differences between
the LD groups in reading skill may reflect a special relationship between deficient
phonological skills and difficulties acquiring good reading skills' (p. 609). Given
the evidence and arguments presented earlier, it seems more likely that Torgesen's
findings support the opposite conclusion, namely, that differences in reading ability are 'driving' differences in phonological processing in working memory. In
support of this suggestion are the results of a follow-up study by Torgesen (1991)
in which a subsample of the original group of LD-N and LD-S children was retested nine years later. Torgesen found that 'children from the LD-S group who
showed relative increases (reduction of the distance between their performance
and that of the LD-N group) in memory span performance from age 10 to 19 read
about as well as the LD-N children' (p. 191). In contrast, the children in the LD-S
group who showed no relative increases in memory span performance over this
period showed almost no improvement in reading skills.

Control Processing in Working Memory

In contrast to the preceding view, which focuses on differences in the
phonological storage and processing component of working memory, the control

processing account ascribes greater importance to differences in the limited capacity central executive that is used to operate control processes in working memory (Tunmer & Hoover, 1992). According to this view, developmental differences in control processing ability (due to maturational delay or cognitive deficit) produce differences in the development of the metalinguistic abilities necessary for acquiring basic decoding skills.

Metalinguistic operations differ from normal language operations in the type of cognitive processing that is required. Normal language processing is modular in nature, involving component operations that are fast, automatic, and largely sealed off from conscious inspection. In contrast, metalinguistic operations require control (or executive) processing, which entails an element of choice in whether or not the operations are performed, as well as relative slowness and deliberateness in the application of such operations. Thus, when comprehending or producing an utterance, language users normally are unaware of the individual phonemes and words comprising the utterance and the grouping relationships among the utterance's constituent words unless they deliberately reflect on the structural features of the utterance.

The relationship between normal language processing and metalinguistic operations can be expressed in terms of a model of sentence comprehension that specifies a set of interacting processes in which the output of each becomes the input to the next (Tunmer & Herriman, 1984; Tunmer, Herriman & Nesdale, 1988). The model provides the basis for a definition of metalinguistic operations in information processing terms as the use of control processing to perform mental operations on the products (i.e. the phonemes, words, sentence structures, and sets of interrelated propositions) of the modular sub-systems involved in sentence comprehension.

Research indicates that metalinguistic development is related to a more general change in information processing capability that occurs during the early stages of middle childhood, which is the development of metacognitive control over the information processing system (Tunmer, 1989; Tunmer, Herriman & Nesdale, 1988; Tunmer & Hoover, 1992). This linkage of metalinguistic development to metacognitive development helps to explain why the ability to treat language as an object of thought is not an automatic consequence of language acquisition. Because the gradual increase in children's control of their cognitive processes does not begin until around four or five years for most children, and even later for some, metalinguistic abilities would not be expected to develop concomitantly with the acquisition of language.

This general framework also provides an explanation for what at first seems rather puzzling; namely, that many five and six year old children who appear to possess normal language comprehension and speaking abilities are nevertheless unable to perform simple metalinguistic operations such as segmenting familiar spoken words into their constituent phonemes, or correcting word order violations in simple sentence structures. The important distinction is that *using* (tacit) knowledge of the grammatical rules of spoken language to construct and comprehend meaningful utterances, which is done intuitively and at a sub-conscious level, is not the same as the metalinguistic act of deliberately performing mental operations *on* the products of the mental mechanisms involved in comprehending and producing utterances.

The claim that the development of metalinguistic ability is related to the development of control processing ability is not to suggest that metalinguistic skills emerge spontaneously in development; that is, without specific stimulation. Children must be exposed to language activities in the home and classroom that focus their attention on the structural features of language. These activities include rhyming and sound analysis games and books that increase phonological sensitivity (e.g. pig Latin, I spy, nursery rhymes, Dr Seuss books), letter games and books that increase letter-name knowledge, games that involve the manipulation of movable letters to form pre-conventional spellings of words, and games and activities that involve listening to and producing 'linguistic' jokes and riddles (i.e. those depending on sound similarity or structural ambiguity). The control processing account therefore proposes that, although some children possess the level of metacognitive ability necessary for acquiring metalinguistic skills, their metalinguistic development may be delayed by inadequate environmental stimulation. Reading development may suffer as a result.

Nevertheless, a significant number of children fail to respond to adequate instruction. As noted earlier, a key question is what causes differences in individual responsiveness to instructional activities, both formal and informal (Stanovich, 1989). For example, research indicates that some children derive little or no benefit from explicit training in metalinguistic abilities. In a large-scale training study of phonological awareness abilities in pre-school children, Lundberg, Frost & Petersen (1988) found that 6% of the children in the training group showed virtually no gains in phonemic segmentation ability, despite having received daily lessons in phonological awareness skills over an eight month period. Similarly, Bradley & Bryant (1985) found that phonological awareness training was helpful for some beginning readers who were not phonologically aware, but not others (see Bryant & Goswami, 1987). As noted earlier, Tunmer, Herriman & Nesdale (1988) found in a longitudinal study that preliterate children who performed very poorly on a phonemic segmentation test at the beginning of first grade varied greatly in phonemic segmentation and phonological recoding ability at the end of the year.

As an explanation of these findings, the control processing account proposes that during the early stages of middle childhood (from four to six years of age), children develop the *capacity* for performing metalinguistic operations when confronted with certain kinds of tasks, such as learning to read (Tunmer, Herriman & Nesdale, 1988). However, as a result of a deficit or developmental delay in metacognition, some children fail to reach the threshold level of control processing ability required to perform the low level metalinguistic operations necessary for developing basic reading skills. Consequently, they will not be able to derive maximum benefit from reading instruction and will be prevented from taking advantage of the reciprocally facilitating relationships between reading achievement and other aspects of development (such as growth in vocabulary, syntactic knowledge, and phonological processing skills), which facilitate further growth in reading. Morais, Alegria & Content (1987) argue along similar lines with regard to the development of phonological awareness:

> The concept of capacity is useful to understanding both at what age appropriate experience may produce the expected effects, and why, given appropriate age and experience, the ability develops in some individuals but not in others. These questions concern the conditions of cognitive development and the problem of learning disabled people. (p. 431)

Most of the research on the relation of metalinguistic development to reading acquisition has focused on phonological awareness (see earlier discussion). More recently, however, researchers have begun to examine the role of syntactic awareness in learning to read. Several studies using a variety of different tasks (e.g. judgement of grammaticality, correction of word order violations or morpheme deletions, oral cloze) have demonstrated that syntactic awareness is related to beginning reading achievement (see Ryan & Ledger, 1984, for a review). Willows & Ryan (1986) found that measures of syntactic awareness were related to beginning reading achievement even when general cognitive ability and vocabulary level were controlled. Using a reading-level match design in which good, younger readers were matched with poor, older readers on reading ability and verbal intelligence, Tunmer, Nesdale & Wright (1987) found that the good readers scored significantly better than the poor readers on two measures of syntactic awareness (an oral cloze task and a word order correction task), suggesting the possibility of a causal connection between syntactic awareness and learning to read. Consistent with these results, Bohannon, Warren-Leubecker & Hepler (1984) found that sensitivity to word-order violations at the beginning of kindergarten, first grade and second grade was strongly related to beginning reading achievement at the end of each grade even when verbal intelligence was held constant.

Tests of syntactic awareness impose processing demands on working memory (as would any metalinguistic task). It is therefore possible that inferior working memory ability rather than deficient metalinguistic ability is the reason why poor readers perform less well on syntactic awareness tasks than good readers. However, Fowler (1988) found that performance on a grammatical error correction task was significantly correlated with reading performance (as measured by pseudoword decoding) even after the effects of verbal working memory had been partialed out. The strength of this relationship ($r = 0.39$) was as great as that between phoneme segmentation and pseudoword decoding ($r = 0.37$), again with the effects of verbal working memory held constant.

As suggested earlier, syntactic awareness may influence reading by helping children acquire phonological recoding skill. When confronted with an unfamiliar word, syntactically aware beginning readers would be able to combine knowledge of the constraints of sentential context with incomplete graphophonemic information to identify the word, and thus increase their knowledge of grapheme–phoneme correspondences. In support of this claim are several studies reporting positive correlations between syntactic awareness and word decoding and/or phonological recoding (Bowey, 1986; Bowey & Patel, 1988; Bryant, MacLean & Bradley, 1990; Fowler, 1988; Siegel & Ryan, 1988; Stanovich, Cunningham & Feeman, 1984; Tunmer, 1989; Tunmer, Herriman & Nesdale, 1988; Willows & Ryan, 1986). Research further indicates that syntactic awareness typically correlates more strongly with context-free word decoding than with reading comprehension (Bowey, 1986; Bowey & Patel, 1988; Siegel & Ryan, 1988; Stanovich *et al.*, 1984; Tunmer, 1989; Willows & Ryan, 1986). And when measures of both word decoding and phonological recoding are included in a study, syntactic awareness usually correlates more highly with phonological recoding. Siegal & Ryan (1988), for example, found that each of three measures of syntactic awareness correlated more strongly with phonological recoding (as measured by pseudoword decoding) than with real word recognition.

It must be emphasised that it is the *combination* of language prediction skills (i.e. syntactic awareness) and emerging phonological recoding skills that provides the basis for acquiring basic reading skills. Language prediction skills will only be useful if they are applied to the problem of breaking the orthographic code. Exclusive reliance on contextual *guessing* to identify unfamiliar words will result in little progress (see Nicholson, this volume; Tunmer & Hoover, 1992, for further discussion). Evidence in support of this claim comes from a study by Evans & Carr (1985) that compared the effects of two instructional approaches (decoding-oriented versus language experience-oriented) on beginning reading achievement. They found that the use of context to make predictions was positively correlated with reading achievement, but only in the group that had received instruction in decoding skills. Evans & Carr concluded from their findings that 'a focus on predictive context utilisation 'worked' in the [decoding-oriented] classrooms because it was combined with print-specific skills taught through word analysis activities, but did not work in the [language experience-oriented] classrooms because the children had few resources for dealing with unfamiliar words' (pp. 343–4).

Although syntactic awareness is clearly related to phonological recoding skill, it must be demonstrated that syntactic awareness makes an *independent* contribution to phonological recoding skill when phonological awareness is included in the analysis. It is possible that syntactic awareness is related to phonological recoding simply because syntactic awareness, like phonological awareness, is a metalinguistic ability and therefore shares in common with phonological awareness many of the same component skills (invoking control processing, performing mental operations on the structural features of language, etc.). However, if syntactic awareness facilitates the development of phonological recoding skill by enabling children to use context to identify unfamiliar words, which, in turn, increases their knowledge of grapheme–phoneme correspondences, then syntactic awareness should make a contribution to the development of phonological recoding skill that is distinct from that made by phonological awareness. In support of this claim are the results of three separate studies by Tunmer and colleagues (Tunmer, 1989; Tunmer, Herriman & Nesdale, 1988; Tunmer & Nesdale, 1986) showing that phonological and syntactic awareness in beginning readers each makes an independent and approximately equal contribution to phonological recoding.

In a recently reported longitudinal study, Bryant, MacLean & Bradley (1990) found strong predictive correlations between measures of phonological and syntactic awareness and later reading achievement. However, in a multiple regression analysis that included three 'extraneous' variables (age at test of reading, mother's educational level, IQ), four linguistic variables (vocabulary, expressive language, receptive language, sentence imitation) and two measures of phonological sensitivity (rhyme and alliteration oddity tasks), syntactic awareness failed to make an independent contribution to future reading achievement. The two phonological sensitivity measures, however, did make independent contributions to reading.

A possible explanation of this finding is that, unlike phonological awareness, syntactic awareness, may also influence the development of listening comprehension by enabling children to monitor their on-going comprehension processes more effectively and to make intelligent guesses about the meanings of unfamiliar words. Syntactic awareness would therefore be expected to be related to aspects of general language development. In the Bryant et al. (1990)

study, syntactic awareness did, in fact, correlate much more highly with the four language measures than did either of the phonological sensitivity measures. This alone would account for the pattern of results obtained by Bryant and colleagues. Consistent with this interpretation, Tunmer (1989) found in a longitudinal study that syntactic awareness was related to later achievement in real word decoding, pseudoword decoding, listening comprehension, and reading comprehension. The same was true for phonological awareness with the exception of *listening* comprehension, where there was no relationship ($r = 0.04$).

In support of the overall control processing account are the results of two longitudinal studies (Tunmer, 1989; Tunmer, Herriman & Nesdale, 1988). In the first study (Tunmer et al., 1988), 118 pre-readers were administered three tests of metalinguistic ability (phonological, syntactic and pragmatic awareness), three pre-reading tests (print awareness, letter identification, and a word recognition test containing frequently occuring sight words), a test of verbal intelligence, and a test of metacognitive control (as measured by tasks requiring decentration ability) at the beginning of first grade. At the end of first grade, the children were re-administered the metalinguistic and pre-reading tests, and three tests of reading achievement (real word decoding, pseudoword decoding, and reading comprehension). The latter tests were re-administered at the end of second grade.

A particularly noteworthy finding was that decentration ability in pre-literate children was more strongly correlated with overall metalinguistic ability at the beginning and end of first grade than was any other school-entry variable. The results further revealed that pre-literate children with low levels of phonological awareness at school entry but above-average levels of decentration ability showed significantly greater improvement in phonological awareness during the school year than children with similarly low levels of phonological awareness but below-average levels of decentration ability at school entry. The mean phonological awareness score of the high-decentration ability group was above the mean of all children's phonological awareness scores at the end of the year, whereas the low-decentration ability group mean was one standard deviation below the overall mean. This finding supports the claim that preliterate children with high levels of decentration ability possess greater cognitive capacity for acquiring the metalinguistic skills necessary for learning to read than do children with low levels of decentration ability.

In the second longitudinal study (Tunmer, 1989), 100 first grade children were administered tests of phonological and syntactic awareness, a test of verbal intelligence, a test of metacognitive control, and four achievement tests (real word decoding, pseudoword decoding, listening comprehension, and reading comprehension). At the end of second grade, these tests were re-administered to 84 children from the original sample.

A path analysis of the data revealed that Grade 1 phonological awareness influenced Grade 2 reading comprehension indirectly through Grade 2 phonological recoding, and that Grade 1 syntactic awareness influenced Grade 2 reading achievement through *both* phonological recoding and listening comprehension. Neither decentration ability (which provided an estimate of metacognitive control) nor verbal intelligence in Grade 1 made an independent contribution to the variability of any of the Grade 2 variables. However, decentration ability made a relatively strong independent contribution to both phonological and syntactic awareness, whereas verbal intelligence made a relatively small independent contribution to syntactic awareness only. Overall, these findings are impressive because they show that metalinguistic abilities in the beginning stages of learning to read are significantly related to later listening and reading achievement, even after the effects of verbal intelligence and decentration ability have been removed. The results further showed that decentration ability was more strongly related to metalinguistic development than was verbal intelligence, as expected.

Concluding Remarks

In this chapter we considered various language-related factors as possible sources of individual differences in the development of word recognition skills. Four different views were presented, each assuming that phonological recoding ability and the ability to perform metalinguistic operations are essential for acquiring basic reading skills. The first focused on general language abilities, the second on specific environmental experiences, the third on phonological processing in working memory, and the fourth on control processing in working memory. On the basis of the research that is currently available, we are inclined to favour an account that emphasises the importance of beginning readers' ability to reflect on and control their strategic processes.

References

Ball, E. and Blackman, B. (1991) Does phoneme awareness training in kindergarten make a difference in early word recognition and developmental spelling? *Reading Research Quarterly* 26, 46–66.
Bisanz, G. L., Das, J. P. and Mancini, G. (1984) Children's memory for phonemically confusable and non-confusable letters: Changes with age and reading ability. *Child Development* 55, 1845–54.
Bohannon, J., Warren-Leubecker, A. and Hepler, N. (1984) Word awareness and early reading. *Child Development* 55, 1541–8.

Bowey, J. A. (1986) Syntactic awareness in relation to reading skill and ongoing reading comprehension monitoring. *Journal of Experimental Child Psychology* 41 282–99.
—   (1990) On rhyme, language and children's reading. *Applied Psycholinguistics* 11, 439–48.
Bowey, J. A. and Patel, R. K. (1988) Metalinguistic ability and early reading achievement. *Applied Psycholinguistics* 9, 367–83.
Bradley, L. and Bryant, P. E. (1978) Difficulties in auditory organisation as a possible cause of reading backwardness. *Nature* 271, 746–7.
—   (1985) *Rhyme and Reason in Reading and Spelling.* Ann Arbor: University of Michigan Press.
Brady, S. A. and Fowler, A. E. (1988) Phonological precursors to reading acquisition. In R. Masland and M. Masland (eds) *Preschool Prevention of Reading Failure* (pp. 204–15). Parkton, MD: York Press.
Bryant, P. E. (1986) Phonological skills and learning to read and write. In B. Foorman and A. Siegal (eds) *Acquisition of Reading Skills: Cultural Constraints and Cognitive Universals* (pp. 51–69). Hillsdale, NJ: Lawrence Erlbaum Associates.
Bryant, P. E. and Bradley, L. (1985) *Children's Reading Problems.* Oxford: Blackwell.
Bryant, P. E. and Goswami, U. (1987) Beyond grapheme-phoneme correspondence. *Cahiers de Psychologie Cognitive* 7, 439–43.
Bryant, P., MacLean, M. and Bradley, L. (1990) Rhyme, language and children's reading. *Applied Psycholinguistics* 11, 237–52.
Byrne, B. (1991) Experimental analysis of the child's discovery of the alphabetic principle. In L. Rieben and C. Perfetti (eds) *Learning to Read: Basic Research and its Implications* (pp. 75–84). Hillsdale, NJ: Lawrence Erlbaum Associates.
—   (1992) Studies in the acquisition procedure for reading: Rationale, hypotheses, and data. In P. B. Gough, L. C. Ehri and R. Treiman (eds) *Reading Acquisition.* (pp. 1–34). Hillsdale, NJ: Lawrence Erlbaum Associates.
Byrne, B. and Fielding-Barnsley, R. (1989) Phonemic awareness and letter knowledge in the child's acquisition of the alphabetic principle. *Journal of Educational Psychology* 81, 313–21.
Chafe, W. (1985) Linguistic differences produced by differences between speaking and writing. In D. Olson, N. Torrance and W. Hildyard (eds) *Literacy, Language and Learning: The Nature and Consequence of Reading and Writing* (pp. 105–23). London: Cambridge University Press.
Ehri, L. C. (1984) How orthography alters spoken language competencies in children learning to read and spell. In J. Downing and R. Valtin (eds) *Language Awareness and Learning to Read* (pp. 119–47). New York: Springer-Verlag.
—   (1986) Sources of difficulty in learning to spell and read. In M. Wolraich and D. K. Routh (eds) *Advances in Developmental and Behavioral Pediatrics* (pp. 121–95). Greenwich, CT: JAI Press.
—   (1987) Learning to read and spell words. *Journal of Reading Behaviour* 19, 5–31.
—   (1989) The development of spelling knowledge and its role in reading acquisition and reading disability. *Journal of Learning Disabilities* 22, 356–65.
Ehri, L. C. and Wilce, L. S. (1980) The influence of orthography on readers' conceptualization of the phonemic structure of words. *Applied Psycholinguistics* 1, 371–85.
Ellis, N. (1990) Reading, phonological skills and short-term memory: Interactive tributaries of development. *Journal of Research in Reading* 13, 107–22.
Ellis, N. and Large, B. (1987) The development of reading: As you seek so shall you find. *British Journal of Psychology* 78, 1–28.

Evans, M. A. and Carr, T. H. (1985) Cognitive abilities, conditions of learning and the early development of reading skill. *Reading Research Quarterly* 20, 327–50.

Fowler, A. E. (1988) Grammaticality judgements and reading skill in Grade 2. *Annals of Dyslexia* 38, 73–94.

Gough, P. B. and Hillinger, M. L. (1980) Learning to read: An unnatural act. *Bulletin of the Orton Society* 30, 179–96.

Gough, P. B. and Juel, C. (1991) The first stages of word recognition. In L. Rieben and C. Perfetti (eds) *Learning to Read: Basic Research and its Implications* (pp. 47–56). Hillsdale, NJ: Lawrence Erlbaum Associates.

Gough, P. B., Juel, C. and Roper-Schneider, D. (1983) Code and cipher: A two-stage conception of initial reading acquisition. In J. A. Niles and L. A. Harris (eds) *Searches for Meaning in Reading/Language Processing and Instruction* (pp. 207–11). Rochester, New York: The National Reading Conference.

Gough, P. B. and Tunmer, W. E. (1986) Decoding, reading and reading disability. *Remedial and Special Education* 7, 6–10.

Hoover, W. A. and Gough, P. B. (1990) The simple view of reading. *Reading and Writing: An Interdisciplinary Journal* 2, 127–60.

Hulme, C. (1981) *Reading Retardation and Multi-Sensory Teaching*. London: Routledge and Kegan Paul.

Johnston, R. S. (1982) Phonological coding in dyslexic readers. *British Journal of Psychology* 73, 455–60.

Johnston, R. S., Rugg, M. D. and Scott, T. (1987) Phonological similarity effects, memory span and developmental reading disorders: The nature of the relationship. *British Journal of Psychology* 78, 205–11.

Jorm, A. F., Share, D. L., MacLean, R. and Matthews, R. (1984) Phonological recoding skills and learning to read: A longitudinal study. *Applied Psycholinguistics* 5, 201–7.

Juel, C., Griffith, P. L. and Gough, P. B. (1986) Acquisition of literacy: A longitudinal study of children in first and second grade. *Journal of Educational Psychology* 78, 243–55.

Liberman, I. Y. and Shankweiler, D. (1985) Phonology and the problem of learning to read and write. *Remedial and Special Education* 6, 8–17.

— (1991) Phonology and beginning reading: A tutorial. In L. Rieben and C. Perfetti (eds) *Learning to Read: Basic Research and its Implications* (pp. 3–17). Hillsdale, NJ: Lawrence Erlbaum Associates.

Liberman, I. Y., Shankweiler, D. and Liberman, A. M. (1989) The alphabetic principle and learning to read. In D. Shankweiler and I. Liberman (eds) *Phonology and Reading Disability: Solving the Reading Puzzle* (pp. 1–33). Ann Arbor, MI: University of Michigan Press.

Lundberg, I., Frost, J. and Petersen, O. (1988) Effects of an extensive program for stimulating phonological awareness in preschool children. *Reading Research Quarterly* 23, 263–84.

Mann, V. A. (1984) Longitudinal prediction and prevention of early reading difficulty. *Annals of Dyslexia* 34, 117–36.

— (1986) Why some children encounter reading problems: The contribution of difficulties with language processing and language sophistication to early reading disability. In J. K. Torgesen and B. Wong (eds) *Psychological and Educational Perspectives on Learning Disabilities* (pp. 133–59). New York: Academic Press.

— (1987) Phonological awareness and alphabetic literacy. *Cahiers de Psychologie Cognitive* 7, 476–81.

Mann, V. A., Cowin, E. and Schoenheimer, J. (1989) Phonological processing, language comprehension and reading ability. *Journal of Learning Disabilities* 22, 76–89.

Mann, V. A. and Liberman, I. Y. (1984) Phonological awareness and verbal short-term memory. *Journal of Learning Disabilities* 17, 592–99.

Morais, J. (1991) Phonological awareness: A bridge between language and literacy. In D. Sawyer and B. Fox (eds) *Phonological Awareness in Reading: The Evolution of Current Perspectives* (pp. 31–71). New York: Springer-Verlag.

Morais, J., Alegria, J. and Content, A. (1987) The relationship between segmental analysis and alphabetic literacy: An interactive view. *Cahiers de Psychologie Cognitive* 7, 415–38.

Morais, J., Cary, L., Alegria, J. and Bertelson, P. (1979) Does awareness of speech as a sequence of phones arise spontaneously? *Cognition* 7, 323–31.

Perfetti, C. A., Beck, I., Bell, L. and Hughes, C. (1987) Phonemic knowledge and learning to read are reciprocal: A longitudinal study of first grade children. *Merrill-Palmer Quarterly* 33, 283–319.

Read, C., Zhang, Y., Nie, H. and Ding, B. (1986) The ability to manipulate speech sounds depends on knowing alphabetic reading. *Cognition* 24, 31–44.

Rohl, M. and Tunmer, W. E. (1988) Phonemic segmentation skill and spelling acquisition. *Applied Psycholinguistics* 9, 335–50.

Ryan, E. and Ledger, G. (1984) Learning to attend to sentence structure: Links between metalinguistic development and reading. In J. Downing and R. Valtin (eds) *Language Awareness and Learning to Read* (pp. 149–71). New York: Springer-Verlag.

Shankweiler, D. and Crain, S. (1986) Language mechanisms and reading disorder: A modular approach. *Cognition* 24, 139–68.

Share, D. L., Jorm, A. F., Maclean, R. and Matthews, R. (1984) Sources of individual differences in reading acquisition. *Journal of Educational Psychology* 76, 1309–24.

Siegel, L. S. and Ryan, E. B. (1988) Development of grammatical-sensitivity, phonological, and short-term memory skills in normally achieving and learning disabled children. *Developmental Psychology* 24, 28–37.

Stanovich, K. E. (1986) Matthew effects in reading: Some consequences of individual differences in the acquisition of literacy. *Reading Research Quarterly* 21, 360–406.

— (1987) Perspectives on segmental analysis and alphabetic literacy. *Cahiers de Psychologie Cognitive* 7, 514–19.

— (1988a) Explaining the difference between the dyslexic and garden-variety poor readers: The phonological-core variable-difference model. *Journal of Learning Disabilities* 21, 590–604.

— (1988b) Science and learning disabilities. *Journal of Learning Disabilities* 21, 210–14.

— (1989) Various varying views on variation. *Journal of Learning Disabilities* 22, 366–9.

— (1991) Discrepancy definitions of reading disability: Has intelligence led us astray? *Reading Research Quarterly* 26, 7–29.

Stanovich, K. E., Cunningham, A. E. and Feeman, D. J. (1984) Intelligence, cognitive skills and early reading progress. *Reading Research Quarterly* 19, 278–303.

Torgesen, J. K. (1988) Studies of children with learning disabilities who perform poorly on memory span tasks. *Journal of Learning Disabilities* 21, 605–12.

— (1991) Cross-age consistency in phonological processing. In S. Brady and D. Shankweiler (eds) *Phonological Processes in Literacy* (pp. 187–93). Hillsdale, NJ: Lawrence Erlbaum Associates.

Tunmer, W. E. (1989) The role of language-related factors in reading disability. In D. Shankweiler and I. Liberman (eds) *Phonology and Reading Disability: Solving the Reading Puzzle* (pp. 91–131). Ann Arbor, MI: University of Michigan Press.

— (1991) Phonological awareness and literacy acquisition. In L. Rieben and C. Perfetti (eds) *Learning to Read: Basic Research and its Implications* (pp. 105–19). Hillsdale, NJ: Lawrence Erlbaum Associates.

Tunmer, W. E. and Herriman, M. L. (1984) The development of metalinguistic awareness: A conceptual overview. In W. E. Tunmer, C. Pratt and M. L. Herriman (eds) *Metalinguistic Awareness in Children: Theory, Research and Implications* (pp. 12–35). New York: Springer-Verlag.

Tunmer, W. E., Herriman, M. L. and Nesdale, A. R. (1988) Metalinguistic abilities and beginning reading. *Reading Research Quarterly* 23, 134–58.

Tunmer, W. E. and Hoover, W. (1992) Cognitive and linguistic factors in learning to read. In P. B. Gough, L. C. Ehri and R. Treiman, (eds) *Reading Acquisition* (pp. 175–214). Hillsdale, NJ: Lawrence Erlbaum Associates.

Tunmer, W. E. and Nesdale, A. R. (1982) The effects of digraphs and pseudowords on phonemic segmentation in young children. *Applied Psycholinguistics* 3, 299–311.

— (1985) Phonemic segmentation skill and beginning reading. *Journal of Educational Psychology* 77, 417–27.

— (1986) Path analysis of the relation of phonological and syntactic awareness to reading comprehension in beginning readers. Unpublished raw data.

Tunmer, W. E., Nesdale, A. R. and Wright, A. D. (1987) Syntactic awareness and reading acquisition. *British Journal of Developmental Psychology* 5, 25–34.

Tunmer, W. E., Pratt, C. and Herriman, M. L. (1984) *Metalinguistic Awareness in Children: Theory, Research and Implications.* New York: Springer-Verlag.

Tunmer, W. E. and Rohl, M. (1991) Phonological awareness and reading acquisition. In D. Sawyer and B. Fox (eds) *Phonological Awareness in Reading: The Evolution of Current Perspectives* (pp. 1–30). New York: Springer-Verlag.

Vellutino, F. R. and Denckla, M. (1991) Cognitive and neuropsychological foundations of word identification in poor and normally developing readers. In R. Barr, M. L. Kamil, P. B. Mosenthal and P. D. Pearson (eds) *Handbook of Reading Research* Vol. 2 (pp. 571–608). New York: Longman.

Vellutino, F. R. and Scanlon, D. M. (1987a) Linguistic coding and reading ability. In S. Rosenberg (ed.) *Advances in Applied Psycholinguistics* Vol. 2 (pp. 1–69). New York: Cambridge University Press.

— (1987b) Phonological coding, phonological awareness and reading ability: Evidence from a longitudinal and experimental study. *Merrill Palmer Quarterly* 33, 321–63.

Wagner, R., Balthazar, M., Hurley, S., Morgan, S., Rashotte, C., Shaner, R., Simmons, K. and Stage, S. (1987) The nature of pre-readers' phonological processing abilities. *Cognitive Development* 2, 355–73.

Willows, D. M. and Ryan, E. B. (1986) The development of grammatical sensitivity and its relationship to early reading achievement. *Reading Research Quarterly* 21, 253–66.

Yopp, H. K. (1988) The validity and reliability of phonemic awareness tests. *Reading Research Quarterly* 23, 159–77.

Appendix: Reading Instruction for the Initial Years in New Zealand Schools

G. BRIAN THOMPSON

From 'Word Experience' to 'Book Experience'

Reading instruction in New Zealand schools is for children from age five years. Children enter school when they reach their fifth birthday, entry taking place throughout the school year. A description is given here of the teaching approach typical in New Zealand for the two to three years following school entry.

A basic premise of the approach for over 40 years has been that reading is a process of obtaining meaning from print. This was explicit in the teacher's manual for the *Janet and John* reading series used throughout the 1950s (Department of Education, 1960: 3, 20). However, at that time, there was an emphasis on experience at the word level. The rate of introduction of new words (not more than three for 50 running words) was a criterion in the construction of text for reading books, as well as meaningfulness. In fact, such was the teacher's anxiety about the child's response to new words that it was common practice to introduce new words in the context of classroom activities involving spoken language and some print experience before the child was exposed to the book text containing those words. However, such 'pre-teaching' practices were no longer recommended with the new *Ready to Read* series (Simpson, 1962: 41–2) introduced to schools in 1963, and have now virtually disappeared.

The previous *Janet and John* reading series was an adaptation (with some additions) of a British publisher's version of a United States series, *Alice and Jerry* (UNESCO, 1984: 38). The new *Ready to Read* (Department of Education, 1962–63) series was written and produced in New Zealand. This work was supervised by an experienced teacher and inspector of schools (Simpson, 1962). There was much consultation with teachers, and texts were trialled in a large number of schools. With this new series there was a shift of emphasis from the word level to the book and story level. This emphasis has become even stronger during the past twenty years, along with an increasing concern that the child is predicting reading responses from the story and sentence contexts. Although the current reading series, introduced in the 1980s and still called *Ready to Read*, is graded into a sequence of nine levels covering the initial two to three years of instruction, there is very little deliberate control of the rate of introduction of new words. Selection is at the story level, not the vocabulary level.

In the 1950s, teaching of word analysis was recommended once the child had established reliable reading responses to several dozen words. This word analysis did not include the child's pronunciation of sounds for isolated letters or other components of words. The child listened to sounds in words with common initial letters, e.g. look, little, let, and common final components, e.g. sat, bat, fat (Department of Education, 1960). This 'receptive phonics' ('implicit phonics') has not received emphasis in the past 30 years. A little occurs when the teacher discusses components of particular words in the context of story texts. Most attention is given to initial sounds of words and only occasionally to final sounds. During the past 20 years there has been increased emphasis on teaching letter names. The most common form of 'word analysis' taught is naming the initial letter of a word and this only after the child has attempted prediction of the word from context. Children receiving reading instruction in New Zealand do not 'sound out' and overtly 'blend' the several sub-syllabic sounds of unfamiliar words. It has been shown, however, that by $6^1/_2$ years of age, without this mode of responding, they do occasionally construct non-lexical (nonsense word) responses to unfamiliar words (Thompson, 1986).

Book Experience: The Current Approach

Books. The current core reading series, *Ready to Read*, was published in 1982-86 to replace the original 1962–63 *Ready to Read* series. As with that series, it was produced by the national Department of Education (1985, 1982–86). However, a large part of the new publication was the result of selection of scripts from a wide range of New Zealand writers. Scripts were also solicited by a public invitation. The main criteria for selecting a script were the judged appeal of the story line to the child readers and the significance of the content to the readers' understanding of their world or themselves (UNESCO, 1984: 43–4). Classroom teachers were consulted about the proposed books and a number of them were printed in preliminary versions for evaluation through teaching trials with pupils (UNESCO, 1984: 44–5; 'Revising Ready to Read', 1981).

All of the texts of the first year (expected average progress) are published as separate small books, one story per book. For the subsequent two years, there is a mix of these 'single titles' and some small collections of texts. There is a total of 40 single titles and seven collections. They include 120 texts which cover a range of genre: fiction, nonfiction, poems, fables, and plays. All texts are amply illustrated (Department of Education, 1982–86). The following are sample excerpts from texts at three different graded levels.

First three pages of text of a single title, *Fun with Mo and Toots*. Each sentence is a caption under an illustration. (This title is for guided reading at the first graded level, or independent reading at the second level.)

I like to dress up.
I like to draw monsters.
I like to ride my bike.

First two pages of text of a single title, *Greedy Cat*. (This title is for shared reading at the first level, or guided reading at the fourth level, or independent reading at the sixth level.)

Mum went shopping
and got some sausages.
Along came Greedy Cat.
He looked in the shopping bag.
Gobble, gobble, gobble,
and that was the end of that.

Mum went shopping
and got some sticky buns.
Along came Greedy Cat.
He looked in the shopping bag.
Gobble, gobble, gobble,
and that was the end of that.

First two pages of text of the story *The Big Bed* in the collection of the same title. (This title is for guided reading at the sixth level.)

Mum and Dad have a big bed.
It is soft and warm.
In the morning,
the children come in —
Sam, Paul, Anna and the baby.
There is room for the dog, too.
And the cat.

But one morning,
Dad wanted to sleep in.
'Out you get! All of you!' he said.

'I can't sleep with you lot
jumping about.'

'Please, Dad,' said Sam.
'We'll keep still.'

'You can't keep still,' said Dad.
'Out!'

The vocabulary of the texts is that which arises from the story. Within stories, particularly at the earlier levels, there is some repetition which restricts the
rate of introduction of new words. Between texts, however, the limited control
of vocabulary results in relatively little communality of vocabulary at the same
graded level.

The *Ready to Read* series is intended to be used in conjunction with a variety of many other books of appropriate reading levels. This is universal practice
in New Zealand schools. Commercial publishers in New Zealand have produced
books to parallel or supplement the core *Ready to Read* series.

Methods of Teaching. There are typically three classes of methods by which
books are used: shared book experience, guided reading, and independent reading.
These methods run concurrently through the teaching programme. Books are
given separate grade levels for each method of teaching use. See the three examples above. Some books are recommended for some methods but not others. While
the teacher handbook (Department of Education, 1985) sets out these methods,
they were already common in classrooms (Penton, 1979). The handbook does not
provide lesson by lesson prescriptions, only guidelines within which teachers are
expected to work out their own implementation for their particular pupils.

The *shared book experience* is an important feature of classroom practice
in New Zealand. A story is read to the class or a small group of children. Copies
of the book may be used by each child to follow the text as the teacher reads.
The teacher's reading may be from a book of greatly enlarged size which the
children can watch as the teacher points to the text as she reads, discussing the
story, discussing predictions about events and words, and where appropriate,
making comments on conventions of print.

In *guided reading*, with a child or group, the teacher introduces the text,
encourages the child to attend to the print, and make predictions about what will
happen in the story. From instances which arise in the children's responses, the
teacher assists the children in learning the conventions of print (including direc-
tional aspects and matching of spoken to print words); in making meaningful
predictions of words from context; and when context fails, assists the child in
obtaining a sound cue for the initial letter of the word. (This sound cue may

derive from the child's knowledge of letter names but may also derive from the teacher directing the child's attention to *listening* to common sounds associated with known print words, e.g. *big*, *baby*.) The teacher engages in interaction with the children to elicit their responses to the message of the text. In using the books comprising one story, children will often move on to a new book within a week, so gaining a wide range of experience of many different books.

Children's breadth of experience is further expanded by *independent reading*. The child always has another book available which is at an easier graded level than that which the child is using under the teacher's guidance. The book is selected by the child from titles covering a wide range of graded levels available in the classroom and also from the school library. The children engage in individual reading of such a book, usually daily, and are encouraged to do this silently. They voluntarily return and select succeeding books. Where necessary the teacher assists the child in selecting a book at a suitable graded level. This independent reading is at a relatively easy level for the child and designed to provide an enjoyable reading experience. It is also an opportunity for the child to practice what has been learnt from the teacher in guided reading (Department of Education, 1985).

Individualisation of instruction is a prominent feature of teaching children in their initial years at school in New Zealand. The practice of children commencing school as they turn five years of age means that there is a demand on teachers to respond to each individual as each commences at varying times during the school year. This is different to the teacher response demanded of a classroom of children who all commence at the same time (UNESCO, 1984: 16–17).

Monitoring of Children's Learning. The above methods are informed by the teacher's monitoring of each child's progress in responding to text. Teachers were provided with an increased understanding of aspects of the reading process and monitoring procedures as the result of an educational programme for practising teachers which commenced in 1976 under the leadership of D. Holdaway, J. Penton and J. Slane (Slane, 1979). This continued for several years to enable nation-wide participation by teachers of 5 to 7-year-olds.

The teacher takes individual records of the child's oral reading of books. As well as obtaining an error rate per running words of text, the teacher attempts to interpret the quality of responses, paying particular attention to whether or not the child is judged to be making sense of the text. The proportion of reading errors which the child spontaneously self-corrects is also believed to be an important diagnostic sign. However, the validity of this belief has been challenged (Thompson, 1981, 1984). The main use of the teacher's monitoring is to match books of an appropriate level to each child. Such monitoring is recommended to take place about once a month. An accuracy rate exceeding 95% (on an unfamiliar text) is recommended for a text suitable for independent reading.

Accuracy rates from 90 to 95% are considered acceptable for guided reading (Department of Education, 1985).

Written Language. While reading tasks take a considerable proportion of school time in the first few years at school in New Zealand, there is also much emphasis on the children expressing themselves in written language. Children generate their own written messages and stories. Some incidental learning of concepts of print and of letter names takes place in the course of these writing activities. It is common for teachers to encourage children in their writing to self-generate spellings from sounds of words ('invented spelling'). There is a belief that knowledge of sound-to-letter correspondences obtained through such spelling experience will spontaneously transfer to become knowledge of letter-to-sound correspondences. However, some evidence which challenges this belief is reported in Chapter 2 of this volume.

The Reading Recovery Programme Developed by M. Clay

M. Clay, Emeritus Professor of Auckland University, has been a leading figure in research on reading in New Zealand. She made research observations on children's responses to the texts of the then new *Ready to Read* series in 1963 and subsequently. She did not, however, develop this reading scheme. Her main influence on regular classroom instruction has been in providing teachers with the understanding and the procedures for making observations of children's reading behaviours, such as those relating to concepts of print, to context and letter cues, and monitoring of appropriate book level (Clay, 1979a). Her work influenced the content of the educational programme for practising teachers referred to above (Clay, 1979b; Slane, 1979).

A sequel to this work was her development of an early intervention programme, Reading Recovery (Clay, 1985), which is designed to accelerate the progress of the children who form the slowest 20% of pupils after twelve months of instruction (sixth birthday in New Zealand). This intervention is individual tutoring during daily withdrawal from the classroom for 30 minutes, continuing for a third or more of the school year. The content of the tutoring is intended to provide a more intensive version of what takes place in the ordinary classroom, using the books of the classroom programme in which the child continues to participate. Hence, the main focus is on obtaining meaning from texts and using context, although it includes a limited amount of work on the child listening for component sounds of words (not pronunciation of components). The programme now operates on a national basis and involves a nationally monitored scheme for training teachers in the Reading Recovery procedures. The programme replaces the previous approach of diagnosis and introduction of remedial work in the child's third or fourth year at school. There are no data available to directly compare long-term outcomes and cost-effectiveness of this early intervention scheme with the previous approach. There are, however, some useful independent evaluations (Glynn *et al.*, 1989; Iversen & Tunmer, 1992) of the effectiveness of the programme over one or two-year periods.

References

Clay, M. M. (1979a) *Reading: the Patterning of Complex Behaviour* 2nd edn. Auckland, New Zealand: Heinemann.
— (1979b) Theoretical research and instructional change: A case study. In L. B. Resnick and P. A. Weaver (eds) *Theory and Practice of Early Reading* Vol. 2 (pp. 149–71). Hillsdale, NJ: Erlbaum.
— (1985) *The Early Detection of Reading Difficulties* 3rd edn. Auckland, New Zealand: Heinemann.
Department of Education (1960) *Reading in the Infant Room: A Manual for Teachers.* Wellington, New Zealand: Government Printer.
— (1962–63) *Ready to Read* (18 book titles and vocabulary chart). Wellington, New Zealand: School Publications Branch, Department of Education.
— (1982–86) *Ready to Read.* (52 book titles, 15 enlarged nursery rhyme cards, explanatory chart and pamphlet for parents). Wellington, New Zealand: School Publications Branch, Department of Education.
— (1985) *Reading in Junior Classes (with Guidelines to the Revised Ready to Read Series).* Wellington, New Zealand: Government Printer.
Glynn, T., Crooks, T., Bethune, N., Ballard, K. and Smith, J. (1989) Reading recovery in context. Report to the New Zealand Department of Education. Dunedin, New Zealand: Otago University.
Iversen, S. and Tunmer, W. E. (1993) Phonological processing skills and the reading recovery program. *Journal of Educational Psychology* 85, 1–14.
Penton, J. (1979) Reading in NZ schools: A survey of our theory and practice. *Set: Research Information for Teachers* (New Zealand Council for Educational Research) No. 2, Item '2.
Revising Ready to Ready (1981, December) *National Education* (New Zealand) 63, 195–9.
Simpson, M. M. (1962) *Suggestions for Teaching Reading in Infant Classes.* Wellington, New Zealand: Department of Education.
Slane, J. (1979) An individual, audiovisual in-service course for teachers. The Early Reading In-Service Course. *Journal of Programmed Learning and Educational Technology* 16 (1), 38–45.
Thompson, G. B. (1981) Individual differences attributed to self-correction in reading. *British Journal of Educational Psychology* 51, 228–9.
— (1984) Self-corrections and the reading process: an evaluation of evidence. *Journal of Research in Reading* 7, 53–61.
— (1986) When nonsense is better than sense: non-lexical errors to word reading tests. *British Journal of Educational Psychology* 56, 216–19.
UNESCO (1984) *Textbooks and Reading Materials: Vol. 1. The Ready to Read Project — the New Zealand Experience.* (Prepared by N. Leckie.) Bangkok: UNESCO Regional Office for Education in Asia and the Pacific.

Index